A touch of
ROOIBOS

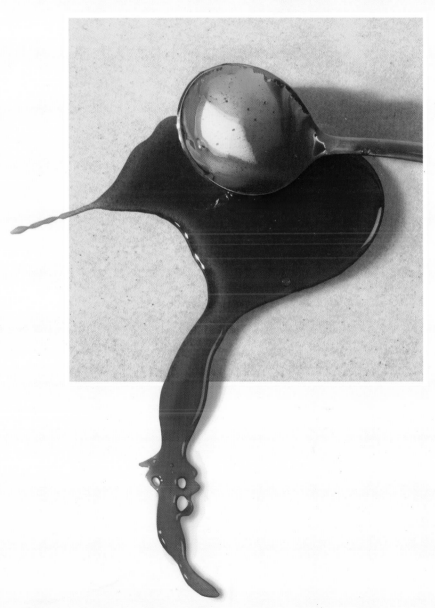

Contents

The Creative Team

This unique book is the result of a wonderful collaboration between a team of like-minded, enthusiastic and creative individuals.

From left: Jeremy Puren (Danie Nel Photography) - Photographer
Karen Hermans (Catapult Advertising Studios) - Designer • Daleen vd Merwe - Editor
Gerda de Wet (Rooibos Limited) - Project Co-ordinator • Kanya Hunt - Stylist • Danie Nel - Photographer

Introduction

Rooibos – a unique and truly South African gift from nature.

The Cederberg Mountains around Clanwilliam is home to Rooibos (Aspalathus linearis) – a versatile plant with a myriad of health-enhancing properties and a thousand uses.

Rooibos Limited approached 14 of South Africa's leading chefs to share some of their creations that include Rooibos as an ingredient. The outcome is this exquisite recipe book that you are holding in your hands right now.

The recipes have been selected to give you a wide choice of dishes, treats and drinks made with ingredients that are easy to source. When you recreate these recipes in your own home, you too will find that a touch of Rooibos really brings out the best in food.

Enjoy every moment of cooking with Rooibos!

ROOIBOS®
LIMITED

The Chefs

Roberto de Carvalho

Working at the Twelve Apostles Hotel & Spa in Cape Town and treating his guests with a true taste of South African cuisine, Roberto loves to experiment with the Fynbos plants and shrubs that grow all around the hotel. He has shown people how to cook with Rooibos in the UK, Singapore, Portugal and Switzerland.

Morné Botha

As Chef at the Giggling Gourmet, Morné has a passion for South African cuisine. He introduced Rooibos to his dishes while he worked as Executive Chef at The Bay Hotel. This proved to be highly popular with foreign and local guests, and spurred him on to explore the use of indigenous ingredients.

Johan Odendaal

As Executive Chef of the award-winning Emily's in Cape Town's Waterfront, Johan contributes greatly to the restaurant's success with his dedicated teaching and innovative cuisine. Johan, who graduated from Stellenbosch University and holds a Culinary Art Institute of Africa Grand Diplôme, is a co-founder of the South African Gourmet Association (SAGA).

Garth Stroebel

Garth is co-owner of and lecturer at the South African Chefs Academy. He is also an accredited judge on the World Association of Chefs Societies' roll and adjudicates at international culinary competitions. Garth has worked at famous hotels such as the Mount Nelson and the Westcliff, and enthusiastically supports South African food.

Reuben Riffel

Reuben has a track record of turning restaurants into award-winning establishments in South Africa and in Britain. As Chef de Cuisine and co-owner of Reuben's Restaurant in Franschhoek, he has won awards for both Chef of the Year and Restaurant of the Year. Reuben's cuisine is eclectic, focusing on the best local and seasonal produce available.

Jaco Slabber

Jaco received his training at Silwood Kitchens in Cape Town before broadening his experience at Rhebokskloof Wine Estate, Zomerluzt Guesthouse, Tredenham Guesthouse and Lita's Restaurant. In 1999, Jaco and his parents took over Olifantshuis Restaurant in Clanwilliam, and this is where he started to experiment with Rooibos in recipes.

Clinton Bonhomme

Clinton has worked in the hospitality industry in South Africa and Britain for 15 years. He is the only pastry chef in the country who has been invited three consecutive times to prepare the dessert for the annual Table of Unity on Table Mountain. He is a Master Patisserie Chef at the Christina Martin School of Food and Wine.

Chantel Dartnall

As Head Chef of Restaurant Mosaic at the Orient Boutique Hotel near Pretoria, Chantel loves to captivate her guests with flavours, textures, and the beauty and elegance of her dishes. Chantel trained under various chefs, including 3-star Michelin chef Nico Ladenis and 2-star Michelin chef Michael Cain in the United Kingdom.

Eric Dyakopu

Born in Mdantsane Township in East London in 1973, Eric discovered his passion for cooking when he started working at Moyo Stellenbosch, Spier Wine Estate, in 2003. He also received his training at Moyo Stellenbosch. Eric is currently heading up the production kitchen and is Moyo Stellenbosch's own authentic tagine, potjie and casserole master.

Malika van Reenen

Malika is the Executive Chef of the Cape Grace Hotel's Signal Restaurant. Her passion for food is inspired by two generations of wonderful cooks – her mother and grandmother. She honed her skills under well-respected chef Mike Bassett, and she explored the culinary scene in London. She studied Hospitality Management.

Luke Dale-Roberts

Luke trained in Zurich, Switzerland, at the luxury Baur au Lac Hotel. He then worked in fine restaurants throughout London before spending five years in Asia, opening restaurants. He now lives in Cape Town with his South African wife and child. He is the Executive Chef of La Colombe Restaurant on the Constantia Uitsig Wine Estate. He was awarded Chef of the year for 2008.

Edgar Osojnik

This Austrian chef gained his experience in the Austrian hospitality industry and at the Grande Roche Relais & Chateaux Hotel in Paarl. He joined Buitenverwachting Restaurant in Constantia, Cape Town, as Chef and partner in 2004, receiving many awards for his cuisine. He holds a Professional Cooking Certificate, and a Food and Beverage Diploma.

Chris Maré

Chris trained under the mentorship of one of SA's top chefs, Mike Basset, and honed his skills at famous institutions such as Cape Town's Ginja Restaurant and the Twelve Apostles Hotel & Spa, and Gauteng's Melrose Arch Protea Hotel. He is now Head Chef at the luxury Bushmans Kloof Wilderness Reserve & Retreat near Clanwilliam.

Philippe Wagenführer

French-born Philippe is the Chef Patron of Roots @ Forum Homini Boutique Hotel outside Johannesburg. He studied at the highly regarded Schiltigheim Catering School in France. Drawing inspiration from the exotic world cities he has worked in, Philippe develops menus which reflect Africa's great diversity.

Other Contributors

Anida van der Spuy

Anida is the heart and frenzy behind the range of Food Frenzy gourmet products. She comes from a professional food and nutrition background, and has 23 years' experience in recipe development, food styling, large-scale catering, lecturing, consulting to hotels and restaurants, and writing for magazines. She has developed various gourmet Rooibos delicacies for Rooibos Ltd.

Kanya Hunt

Kanya thought her passion for food could be satisfied by a BSc in Dietetics, but it wasn't. After 13 years as a therapeutic dietitian she set up her own business baking "the best chocolate and dessert-style wedding cakes". She is also a food stylist who has won several Galliova Awards.

Kevin Snyman

LiquidChefs Pty (Ltd)
Run by young South African entrepreneurs and introducing a new cocktail culture to the world, LiquidChefs is a vibrant, funky company that has changed the concept of portable cocktail bars and bar services. LiquidChefs caters for private functions and large-scale events, and provides consulting services to major corporates and beverage companies.

Cape Town Hotel School

Mariëtte Hattingh

Holding a National Diploma in Food Service Management and a BTech degree, Mariëtte started her career in the catering industry. She has been lecturing at the Cape Town Hotel School for the past 15 years, focusing on pastry, basic skills and competition work. She is studying for a Master's degree in Tourism and Hospitality.

Nina Septoe

Nina's expertise is underpinned by a Food Service Management Diploma, a stint in England, and training under George Jardine at Cellars-Hohenort in Constantia, and at The River Café on Uitsig Wine Estate. She has joined the Cape Town Hotel School as a culinary lecturer, and completed her Master's in Food and Nutrition.

Jerome Peters

Holding a Diploma in Culinary and Hospitality Management, Jerome worked for leading hotels such as the Mount Nelson, Cellars-Hohenort and Sun City. Jerome was invited to become part of the opening team for Jardine Restaurant, having been mentored by George Jardine during the early part of his career. Jerome joined the Cape Town Hotel School after getting married.

Sarah Withey

After graduating from Silwood Kitchens in 1995, Sarah went overseas for a year before coming back to work at ...and Lemon and later Poplars Restaurant. In 2003, she started her own deli and catering company which she ran for three years before taking up a position as Chef Lecturer at the Cape Peninsula University of Technology.

Cooking with Rooibos

Rooibos is ideal in food preparation – simply use it as a substitute for water or milk in any recipe. Rooibos complements and intensifies the natural flavours of food. It is also a natural tenderiser, which makes it a perfect base for meat and chicken marinades.

Apart from being a healthy and refreshing drink in its own right, it is perfect for diluting fruit juices or concentrates.

The mineral content of Rooibos also supplements the nutritional value of food and drinks. Rooibos contains several essential minerals our bodies need, such as calcium, potassium, magnesium, iron, zinc and sodium, as well as the trace elements copper and manganese. The flavonoids and tannins in Rooibos are proven anti-oxidants that help the body fight free radicals.

Rooibos is completely pure and naturally caffeine free.

HOW TO PREPARE ROOIBOS FOR USE IN RECIPES
Different recipes will require different strengths of Rooibos. Use these guidelines to prepare Rooibos according to your taste:

VERY STRONG ROOIBOS
12 Rooibos tea bags in 500 ml boiling water, allow to infuse for 15 minutes.

STRONG ROOIBOS
6 Rooibos tea bags in 500 ml boiling water, allow to infuse for 15 minutes.

MEDIUM-STRENGTH ROOIBOS
3 Rooibos tea bags in 500 ml boiling water, allow to infuse for 15 minutes.

HOW TO SMOKE MEAT WITH ROOIBOS TEA LEAVES
You can either smoke meat – such as chicken, ostrich, duck or springbok – in a smoker or in a saucepan on the stove.

STOVE-TOP METHOD
1. Place Rooibos tea leaves in a large saucepan that has been heated.
2. Set the stove on high.
3. Insert a rack (e.g. a cooling rack) into the saucepan and place the meat on the rack.
4. When the Rooibos is really smoking, cover tightly with a lid, foil or another saucepan, inverted.
5. Turn off the heat, as you do not want an overpowering smoky flavour.
6. Allow to smoke for 7 to 10 minutes.

HINTS AND TIPS
- Replace the liquid in stews and casseroles with Rooibos. It adds a rich aroma and it also tenderises the meat.
- Add Rooibos to sauces and soups for extra flavour, or use it to dissolve stock cubes.
- Store Rooibos tea bags or leaves in an airtight container. Rooibos can be kept for a long period without losing its colour or taste.
- Keep prepared Rooibos in the fridge for later use.

Soups

Remember the reassuring flavours coming from the kitchen when there was a pot of hearty soup simmering on the stove in the middle of winter?

In these rugged mountains of the Cederberg, soup is soul food, comfort food ...

Curried Fish Soup

Morné Botha

4 small whole fish (Ask the fishmonger to fillet and skin the fish for you, and request the head, bones and skin for the fish stock.)
salt to taste
freshly ground black pepper to taste
8 Rooibos tea bags
1,5 litres boiling water
30 ml butter
30 ml sunflower oil
2 onions, finely chopped
2 carrots, peeled and finely chopped
3 sticks celery, finely chopped
3 cloves garlic, sliced
3 cm piece ginger, sliced
10 ml curry powder
1 red chilli, sliced
good pinch saffron strands, soaked in a little warm milk
1 tin (410 g) whole peeled tomatoes, chopped and juices retained
250 ml white wine
4 large potatoes, peeled and finely diced

1. Rinse the head, bones and skin.
2. Cut the fish fillets into 3 x 3 cm pieces, and season with salt and pepper.
   Keep in the fridge until needed.
3. Steep the Rooibos tea bags in the boiling water for 5 minutes. Remove the tea bags.
4. Heat the butter and sunflower oil in a large saucepan. Add the onions, carrots, celery, garlic and ginger and sauté until golden brown. Add the curry powder, chilli, saffron, tinned tomatoes, wine, prepared Rooibos, the fish heads, bones and skin. Cover and simmer for about 15 minutes (the fish eyes should turn white and hard).
5. Remove and discard the heads, bones and skin. Add the diced potatoes, and season with salt and pepper to taste. Return to the boil until the potatoes are cooked and soft, about 8 minutes. Add the seasoned fish pieces and cook for about 5 to 6 minutes or until the fish is cooked.
6. Serve the soup with chunky bread and butter.

Serves 6

Butternut-Rooibos Soup

Edgar Osojnik

1 litre water
3 Rooibos tea bags
1 kg butternut, halved and seeds removed
1 clove garlic, sliced
olive oil
1 medium onion, finely sliced (100 g)
500 ml cream
salt and freshly ground black pepper

1. Pour the water into a medium-sized saucepan, add the Rooibos tea bags and bring to the boil. Simmer for 5 minutes, then remove from the heat and leave the Rooibos to infuse for 20 minutes. Remove the tea bags.
2. Preheat the oven to 180 ºC.
3. Place the halved butternut on a roasting pan, sprinkle with the garlic and a drizzle of olive oil, and roast until soft.
4. Heat a little olive oil in a large saucepan and sauté the onion until soft and translucent.
5. Add the roasted butternut flesh to the onion, and cook for approximately 5 minutes.
6. Add the Rooibos stock and simmer for 30 minutes, stirring occasionally.
7. Add the cream and simmer for 10 minutes (do not allow to boil).
8. Season to taste and mix well.

Serves 4

Vegetable Soup

Chris Maré

500 g dry haricot beans
8 beef stock cubes, dissolved in 3 litres hot, strong Rooibos
250 g bacon, diced
2 cloves garlic, crushed
1 medium onion, chopped
2 stalks of celery, sliced
1 carrot, sliced
5 ml dried rosemary
30 ml tomato paste
½ small head of cabbage, sliced
2 leeks, sliced
3 baby marrows, sliced
5 ml dried sweet basil
50 ml fresh parsley, chopped
1 whole clove
salt to taste
coarsely ground black pepper to taste

1. Wash the beans, place in a large saucepan and cover with the Rooibos stock.
2. Bring to the boil and boil for 5 minutes. Remove from heat and soak for an hour.
3. Bring to the boil again and simmer for 2 hours or until the beans are tender.
4. Drain the beans, reserving the liquid.
5. Purée half the beans in a food processor.
6. Fry the bacon in a pan, add the garlic, onion, celery, carrot and rosemary, and sauté for 5 minutes.
7. Add the rest of the ingredients as well as the liquid, the beans and bean purée.
8. Simmer for 30 minutes.
9. Serve very hot with home-made health bread. (See page 160 for Rooibos Health Bread.)

Serves 8 to 10

Bushmans Kloof, Cederberg

Cream of Corn Soup

Bushmans Kloof for Rooibos Limited

1 tin (410 g) sweetcorn
2 chicken stock cubes, dissolved in 600 ml hot, strong Rooibos
600 ml milk
1 onion, chopped
4 black peppercorns
60 g (65 ml) butter
70 g (125 ml) cake flour
30 ml sherry
sour cream for garnishing
chopped chives for garnishing

1. Simmer the corn and Rooibos stock over low heat for 20 minutes.
2. Pour into a food processor and mix until smooth (or rub through a sieve).
3. Heat the milk with the onion and black peppercorns.
   Pour the milk through a sieve into the corn mixture.
4. Melt the butter in a saucepan. Add the flour and stir to make a smooth paste.
5. Add the corn mixture slowly, stirring constantly.
   Bring to the boil. Add more milk if the soup is too thick.
6. Add the sherry and stir.
7. Garnish with the sour cream and chives to serve.

Serves 4

Bushmans Kloof, Cederberg

Chilled Tomato Soup

Bushmans Kloof for Rooibos Limited

500 g ripe tomatoes, peeled and chopped
250 ml tomato juice
½ container (200 g) pimento*, chopped
430 ml cold, strong Rooibos
1 onion, chopped
12 ml sunflower oil
10 ml brown vinegar
1 clove garlic, crushed
salt to taste
freshly ground black pepper to taste
curry powder to taste
30 ml fresh cream

1. Purée the tomatoes, tomato juice, pimento, Rooibos, onion, oil,
   vinegar and garlic in a food processor until smooth.
2. Flavour with salt, pepper and curry powder.
3. Chill well.
4. Stir in the cream just before serving.

Serves 6 to 8

* Pimento is canned red sweet peppers available bottled or tinned. For this recipe 2 roasted and
  skinned red peppers can also be used instead.

Starters

Starter dishes on a dinner table are like ice-breakers in a conversation — they set the mood, they create interest, they get people talking and sharing ...

Rooibos-Smoked Ostrich Carpaccio*

Chris Maré

CARPACCIO

6 Rooibos tea bags
700 g ostrich fillet
100 ml Cajun spice
100 ml fresh coriander leaves, finely chopped
200 g rocket leaves
50 g Parmesan shavings

ASIAN DRESSING

50 ml soy sauce
15 ml sesame oil
50 ml olive oil
20 ml honey
10 ml pickled ginger, chopped
10 ml fresh coriander, chopped
1 clove garlic, finely chopped
5 g nori sheets, finely chopped (optional)

CARPACCIO

1. Cut open the Rooibos tea bags and sprinkle the leaves over the base of a large saucepan that has a lid. Set on the stove on a high heat.
2. Place a cooling rack on top of the saucepan. Slice the ostrich fillet into strips about 8 cm thick and place on the rack. When the Rooibos is really smoking, cover the meat with the lid.
3. Turn off the heat, as you don't want to overpower the ostrich with the smoky flavour. Leave to stand for about 10 minutes.
4. On a cutting board, mix the Cajun spices and chopped coriander. Remove the ostrich fillet from the rack and roll it in the mixture. Roll up tightly in plastic wrap to form even sausage shapes. Place in the freezer.
5. When frozen, remove and slice into thin slices. Arrange neatly on 4 round plates.

ASIAN DRESSING

6. Place all the dressing ingredients in a food processor and blend until well mixed. Pour into a bottle and store in the refrigerator.
7. Top the ostrich carpaccio with the rocket, Parmesan shavings and Asian dressing.

Serves 4

* Carpaccio is an Italian dish, originally made of paper-thin slices of raw beef that is served cold with a creamy salad dressing or with olive oil and lemon juice. Now carpaccio may refer to any meat or fish that is sliced thinly and served raw.

Pan-Fried Duck Liver with Quince & Mushroom Served with a Rooibos Reduction

Luke Dale-Roberts

QUINCES
1 litre white wine
130 g (150 ml) castor sugar
4 Rooibos tea bags
1 vanilla pod
100 ml granadilla or raspberry vinegar
250 ml muscatel
1 kg quinces, peeled, cored and cut in quarters

DUCK LIVER
400 g duck livers
salt and freshly ground black pepper
30 ml olive oil
200 g large oyster mushrooms
6 bread crisps for garnishing
200 g baby salad leaves or wild rocket

QUINCES

1. Heat the wine, sugar, Rooibos tea bags, vanilla, vinegar and muscatel over low heat and stir until the sugar has dissolved. Strain to remove the tea bags and vanilla pod.
2. Add the quince quarters, bring to the boil and poach until soft. Remove the quinces with a slotted spoon and let them cool.
3. Boil the liquid until it is reduced to a syrup consistency, and keep aside.

DUCK LIVER

4. Season the livers with salt and pepper to taste.
5. Heat the olive oil in a pan over medium to high heat and fry the livers until golden brown on the outside but still just pink inside. Remove the livers from the pan and keep aside.
6. Toss the mushrooms in the same pan until just cooked.

SERVING

7. Dice the cooked quinces. Spoon 3 small piles of the quinces per plate on 6 rectangular plates. Place a duck liver on top of each quince pile. Drizzle with the Rooibos reduction and garnish with bread crisps. Scatter the mushrooms around and finish with baby salad leaves.

NOTES:
• To make thin bread crisps: Half freeze the bread and then slice it into very thin slices. Drizzle with olive oil and bake for about 20 minutes at 130 °C or until golden brown and crisp.
• Chicken livers can also be used for this recipe.

Serves 6

Chicken Liver Parfait

Johan Odendaal

500 g chicken livers
125 ml milk
25 ml port or muscatel*
25 ml Rooibos liqueur
15 ml brandy
12 Rooibos tea bags
3 sprigs of thyme
500 ml cream
3 extra-large eggs
yolks of 5 extra-large eggs
salt
freshly ground black pepper
3 ml cayenne pepper
1 ml saltpeter**
125 ml strong Rooibos

1. Wash the chicken livers under running tap water. Pat dry.
2. Heat the milk until lukewarm and pour over the chicken livers. Allow to stand for 30 minutes.
3. Drain and then rinse the livers gently in cold running water. Pat dry. Remove the membranes, if necessary. Transfer to a mixing bowl.
4. Combine the port, Rooibos liqueur, brandy, 6 of the Rooibos tea bags and the thyme. Pour over the livers. Cover with plastic wrap and marinate for 24 hours (or overnight) in the refrigerator.
5. In a saucepan, heat the cream with the remaining 6 Rooibos tea bags over high heat to boiling point. Reduce the heat and stir until the cream has reduced by half. Allow to cool down. Remove the tea bags.
6. Preheat the oven to 150 ºC.
7. Remove the livers from the refrigerator. Strip the leaves from the sprigs of thyme. Transfer the livers, marinade, thyme leaves and cream mixture to a food processor and blend until smooth. Keeping the machine running, add the eggs and egg yolks one at a time. Continue blending for a further minute after the last addition. Pass the mixture through a sieve into a clean mixing bowl.
8. Season to taste with salt, pepper and cayenne pepper. Add the saltpeter and Rooibos. Mix well. Adjust seasoning if necessary.
9. Pour the mixture into a lined, flat baking pan and place in a larger pan, half-filled with water. Bake for 30 to 40 minutes, until the mixture is just set and firm to the touch. Open the oven door, switch the oven off and leave the chicken-liver mixture to cool in the oven.
10. Remove the parfait from the oven and cover with plastic wrap. Refrigerate until needed.
11. Cut the parfait into rectangles and serve with Rooibos Raisin Bread (see page 158) and Rooibos Dressing (see page 196).

Serves 12

 * Port is a fortified wine originally from Portugal. Brandy is added to the wine when it is half fermented. Muscatel is a dessert wine made from Muscat grapes.

** Saltpeter is also called potassium nitrate and is available from pharmacies. The saltpeter keeps the livers pink.

Rooibos-Scented Gravadlax* of Salmon

Philippe Wagenführer

ROOIBOS CURING MIX
100 ml Rooibos tea leaves
10 ml honey
juice of 1 lemon
finely grated zest of 5 lemons
10 coriander seeds, crushed
200 g (250 ml) brown sugar
100 g (90 ml) coarse sea salt

SALMON AND DRESSING
500 g thick salmon fillet, skin on
500 g cucumber (use a large cucumber)
10 ml coarse sea salt
100 ml Rooibos tea leaves
100 ml water
30 ml honey
juice of 1 lemon
finely grated zest of 5 lemons

ROOIBOS CURING MIX

1. Blend the Rooibos tea leaves, honey, lemon juice, zest and coriander seeds in a food processor to form a fine paste. Mix the sugar and the salt together. Add to the paste and mix well.

SALMON AND DRESSING

2. Rub the paste on the top of the salmon fillet. Place a weight on top of the fish and leave it to stand for 12 hours in the fridge to cure.
3. The next day, drain the juices off. Keep the Rooibos curing mixture on top of the salmon.
   Remove the skin and cut the fish into 3 cm thick slices.
4. Peel the cucumber, remove the seeds and cut into large cubes.
   Salt the cubes and leave to steep for 1 hour.
5. To make the dressing, heat the Rooibos tea leaves and water in a saucepan to form a strong brew.
   Add the honey, lemon juice and zest. Add more seasoning, if necessary.
   Pour through a fine-mesh sieve to remove the solids. Set the dressing aside.
6. Rinse the cucumber under cold water, drain in a sieve and dry on kitchen paper to discard the liquid.
7. To serve, place the salmon fillets and cucumber cubes on plates. Drizzle with the Rooibos dressing.

Serves 4

* Gravadlax (also known as gravlax or gravlaks) is raw salmon cured with salt, sugar, a spirit such as vodka, peppercorns and flavoured with dill.

Rooibos Prawn & Apple Surprise

Eric Dyakopu

SAUCE
40 ml butter
2 onions, finely chopped
250 ml fresh cream
2 pinches saffron
10 ml honey
10 ml Dijon mustard
50 ml very strong Rooibos
¼ each red, green and yellow pepper, cut in thin strips
salt and freshly ground black pepper to taste

PRAWNS
2 Rooibos tea bags
24 extra-large prawns,
   shelled and deveined
3 apples, cut in quarters
30 ml butter
2 handfuls wild rocket for garnish
2 fresh limes, sliced

SAUCE

1. Heat the butter in a small saucepan and sauté the onions until soft.
2. Add the cream, saffron, honey, mustard and Rooibos, and simmer until thick.
   Add the peppers and season with salt and pepper to taste.

PRAWNS

3. Half-fill a saucepan with water and bring to the boil. Add the Rooibos tea bags and prawns
   and poach until the prawns are just cooked.
4. Remove the prawns with a slotted spoon and add to the sauce.
5. Poach the apple quarters in the same Rooibos for a few minutes. They must not be too soft.
   Remove the apples from the liquid and sauté in the butter until lightly browned.
6. Place 3 apple quarters per plate in the centre of 4 plates and top with the prawns.
   Pour the sauce over and garnish with the rocket. Serve with fresh lime slices.

Serves 4

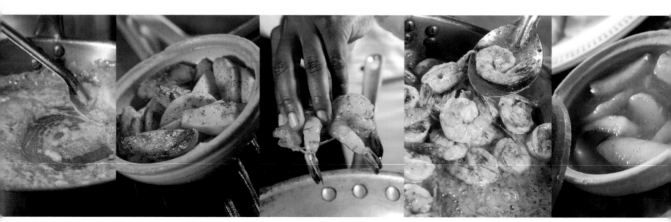

Rooibos & Ginger-Cured Beef Carpaccio

Malika van Reenen

200 g (250 ml) sugar
280 g (250 ml) coarse rock salt
50 ml Rooibos tea leaves
100 g fresh ginger, finely chopped
15 ml black pepper
zest of 1 orange
1 kg beef fillet or sirloin, trimmed
30 ml Dijon mustard
30 ml chopped fresh parsley
fresh rocket
Parmesan cheese shavings
olive oil for dressing

1. Mix the sugar, salt, Rooibos tea leaves, ginger, pepper and orange zest together.
2. Place the beef in a small roasting tray and pack with the salt mixture.
   Leave to cure for 2 to 3 hours.
3. Rinse off the curing salt and dry the meat with kitchen paper. Spread the mustard and chopped
   parsley over the beef. Roll the beef tightly in plastic wrap and place in the freezer.
4. When needed, remove the plastic wrap and slice the beef into very thin slices.
   Serve with fresh rocket and shaved Parmesan cheese and drizzle with olive oil.

Serves 8

Black Mushrooms Stuffed with Rooibos Risotto, with Salad Greens and Whipped Parmesan Cream

Sarah Withey

ROOIBOS RISOTTO
180 g (200 ml) butter
1½ onions, finely chopped
2 cloves garlic, crushed
600 ml Arborio rice
3 litres medium-strength Rooibos
70 ml grated Parmesan cheese
200 g red peppers, finely diced
45 ml chopped fresh parsley
salt and freshly ground black pepper
8 large black mushrooms
fresh herbs to garnish

SALAD
400 g mixed baby lettuce leaves
30 ml olive oil
30 ml white wine vinegar
salt and freshly ground black pepper
24 cherry tomatoes, halved

PARMESAN CREAM
400 ml cream
100 ml finely grated Parmesan cheese

ROOIBOS RISOTTO

1. Heat 90 g (100 ml) of the butter in a large saucepan and sauté the onions and garlic until translucent.
2. Add the rice and fry for 5 minutes, stirring from time to time to coat the rice with the butter.
3. Heat the Rooibos until boiling. Slowly add the warm Rooibos, a cup at a time, to the rice mixture. Stir well after each addition and simmer until the liquid has been absorbed completely before adding the next cupful. Continue adding the warm Rooibos until the rice is cooked (al dente) and the mixture creamy.
4. Add the Parmesan cheese, red peppers, parsley and the rest of the butter (90 g). Season with salt and pepper to taste.
5. Peel the mushrooms. Heat a little olive oil in a frying pan and sauté the mushrooms until they start to soften. Remove from the pan and place, cap side down, in an ovenproof dish.
6. Fill the centre of the mushrooms with the risotto. Just before serving, drizzle the mushrooms with a little olive oil and place in the oven until warmed through.

SALAD

7. Place all the leaves in a bowl, and dress with the olive oil, vinegar, salt and pepper.

PARMESAN CREAM

8. Whisk the cream until firm, fold in the Parmesan cheese and season to taste.

SERVING

9. To serve, place a small handful of salad leaves in the centre of a plate, and top with a warmed mushroom and risotto. Place the halved cherry tomatoes beside the black mushroom. Place a spoonful of Parmesan cream on top of the risotto. Garnish with fresh herbs.

Serves 8

Salads

"It's difficult to think anything but pleasant thoughts while eating a home-grown tomato."

- Lewis Grizzard

Rooibos-Smoked Duck Breast Salad

Jaco Slabber

10 ml ground cinnamon
10 ml masala
5 ml finely chopped chillies
60 ml honey
20 ml olive oil
salt to taste
freshly ground black pepper to taste
4 duck breasts
250 g Rooibos tea leaves
fresh cream to taste
200 g mixed baby lettuce leaves
cherry tomatoes, halved
mango atchar

1. In a shallow bowl, mix the cinnamon, masala, chillies, honey, oil, salt and pepper.
   Make some incisions into the skin of the duck breasts. Place the duck breasts in the mixture,
   turning to coat completely. Cover and marinate overnight.
2. Place the loose Rooibos tea leaves in a smoker*, place the duck breasts above the leaves
   and smoke over a medium heat for approximately 20 minutes.
3. Pour the marinade into a saucepan and bring to the boil.
   Remove from the heat and stir in the cream to taste.
4. Slice the duck breasts and serve on a handful of lettuce leaves and some cherry tomatoes,
   topped with the sauce and mango atchar.

Serves 4

* See page 10 to smoke the duck without a smoker.

Rooibos-Marinated Chicken Salad with Avocado & Red Chilli, and Rooibos & Lemon Vinaigrette

Reuben Riffel

2 chicken breasts, without skin or bones
30 ml coarse sea salt
1 tin (400 ml) coconut milk
375 ml strong Rooibos
30 ml castor sugar
1 red chilli, deseeded
125 ml fresh mint leaves
1 clove garlic, chopped
juice of 1 lemon
125 ml canola oil
125 ml mixed baby salad leaves
125 ml bean or onion sprouts
3 cherry tomatoes, halved
1 spring onion, sliced
1 avocado

1. Rub the chicken breasts with the sea salt and place in the refrigerator for 1 hour.
2. Preheat the oven to 150 °C.
3. Place the coconut milk, 250 ml of the Rooibos and 15 ml of the castor sugar in a shallow roasting pan. Submerge the chicken breasts in the coconut milk mixture.
4. Bake for 20 minutes or until the chicken is cooked.
5. Remove the pan from the oven and leave to cool. Remove the chicken from the liquid and refrigerate until completely cooled. (Reserve the coconut milk mixture for a soup, sauce for fish or a warm noodle dish.)
6. To make the dressing, place the chilli, 2 mint leaves, garlic and a little sea salt in a mortar or small bowl. Pound to a smooth paste. Add the lemon juice, remaining Rooibos, the remaining castor sugar and the canola oil. Mix well.
7. To assemble, cut the cold chicken into thin strips. Toss together the remaining mint leaves, salad leaves, sprouts, tomatoes, spring onion and sliced chicken. Cube the avocado and place in a mound in the centres of two plates. Add the dressing to the salad mixture and place the salad mixture on top of the avocado. Top with a little extra dressing.

Serves 2

Grilled Pear Salad with Rooibos Garam Masala Syrup

Roberto de Carvalho

500 ml strong Rooibos
100 g (125 ml) sugar
1 piece cinnamon stick, about 5 cm
2 pieces fresh ginger (about 2,5 x 0,5 cm each), crushed
10 ml green or white cardamom pods, lightly crushed
10 ml coriander seeds, lightly crushed
10 whole black peppercorns, lightly crushed
1 ml Garam Masala powder
60 ml raw green pumpkin seeds (not roasted)
salt
2 Asian pears (or normal pears)
60 ml fresh lemon juice
about 4 x 250 ml mixed baby greens, such as baby rocket, tatsoi, red baby spinach
salt and freshly ground black pepper

1. Place the Rooibos, sugar, cinnamon stick, ginger, cardamom, coriander seeds, peppercorns and Garam Masala powder in a large, heavy-based saucepan. Bring to the boil. Stir until the sugar is dissolved.
2. Reduce the heat and simmer for about 15 minutes until the syrup is reduced to about 125 ml. Remove from the heat. Cover and set aside for about 1 hour to allow the flavours to infuse. Strain the syrup through a sieve into a bowl, discarding the solids.
3. Heat a large, heavy-based frying pan or grill pan over moderate heat until hot. Toast the pumpkin seeds, stirring constantly, for 3 to 5 minutes until puffed and beginning to pop. Transfer the seeds to a plate and season with salt.
4. Halve and core the pears. Cut into wedges and drizzle with lemon juice. Grill the pear wedges on a hot grill pan on each side until there are grill lines on all sides. Place the pears into the syrup. Drain the pears, reserving the syrup.
5. Toss the baby salad greens with the syrup reserved from the pears. Season to taste with salt and pepper.
6. To serve, mound the greens and pear wedges on 4 plates. Sprinkle with the pumpkin seeds. Drizzle some of the reserved syrup around each salad.

NOTES:
• The syrup can be made up to 1 week in advance and chilled in a sealed container.
• The salad is also good served with slivers of fresh avocado (in season) and a slice of toasted baguette with pesto.
• The combination of sweet Rooibos and spicy Garam Masala in the syrup adds so much flavour to this refreshing salad that no oil is necessary.

Serves 4

Roasted Asparagus with Rooibos-Naartjie Dressing

Roberto de Carvalho

450 g asparagus, trimmed
5 ml extra-virgin olive oil
2 large naartjies or small oranges
80 ml fresh naartjie or orange juice
45 ml Rooibos syrup (see Baklava with Rooibos Syrup, page 116)
10 ml rice vinegar
8 ml oriental sesame oil
8 ml naartjie or orange zest, grated
1 clove garlic, crushed
3 ml fresh ginger, peeled and grated
salt
freshly ground black pepper
30 ml finely chopped spring onion tops
30 ml finely chopped roasted peanuts

1. Preheat the oven to 220 °C. Place the asparagus in a medium-sized bowl and pour enough cold water over to cover. Leave to stand for 15 minutes. Drain.
2. Arrange the asparagus in a baking dish (about 33 x 23 x 5 cm) and drizzle with the olive oil. Roast for about 10 minutes. Turn occasionally, until the asparagus is crisp-tender. (Alternatively the asparagus and nuts can be sautéed in a frying pan.) Transfer to a platter and set aside to cool.
3. Using a sharp knife, cut the peel and white pith from the naartjies. Cut between the membranes to release the segments. Arrange the naartjie segments on top of the asparagus.
4. To make the dressing, whisk the naartjie juice, Rooibos syrup, vinegar, sesame oil, naartjie zest, garlic and ginger together in small bowl. Season the mixture to taste with salt and pepper. Drizzle the dressing over the asparagus and naartjies. Sprinkle with spring onion tops and peanuts and serve.

Serves 4

Sweet Potato Salad with Rooibos-Orange Dressing

Roberto de Carvalho

60 ml extra-virgin olive oil
30 ml Rooibos syrup (see Baklava with Rooibos Syrup, page 116)
30 ml orange juice
30 ml sherry vinegar or balsamic vinegar
15 ml fresh lemon juice
10 ml fresh ginger, peeled and crushed
2 ml ground cinnamon
1 ml ground nutmeg
salt
freshly ground black pepper
2,5 kg red-skinned sweet potatoes, peeled and cut into 2 cm cubes
250 ml spring onions, chopped
250 ml fresh parsley, chopped
100 g (250 ml) pecan nuts, toasted and coarsely chopped
65 g (125 ml) sultanas
65 g (125 ml) raisins

1. To make the dressing, whisk the olive oil, Rooibos syrup, orange juice, vinegar, lemon juice, ginger, cinnamon and nutmeg together in small bowl. Season to taste with salt and pepper.
2. To make the salad, steam the sweet potatoes in batches for about 10 minutes per batch until just tender. Transfer the sweet potatoes to a large bowl.
   Set aside to cool to room temperature.
3. Add the spring onions, parsley, pecan nuts, sultanas and raisins.
   Pour the dressing over the top and toss gently to blend.
   Season to taste with salt and pepper.

NOTE:
The salad can be made up to 2 hours before serving. Leave to stand at room temperature.

Serves 12

Main Dishes

*We should never eat because we're hungry.
We should eat to feed our bodies
and our souls, and to feel nurtured by food
that's been made with love.*

Grilled Crayfish with Rooibos Butter

Morné Botha

250 ml white wine
250 ml strong Rooibos
2 sprigs thyme
125 ml flat-leaf parsley, finely chopped
2 cloves garlic, finely chopped
1 red onion, finely chopped
500 g (550 ml) butter, softened
juice and zest of 2 lemons
juice and zest of 2 oranges
15 ml paprika
80 ml brandy
100 g Dijon mustard
3 egg yolks
4 x 800 g live crayfish, placed in the freezer for about 1 hour to stun them, and to make handling easier
salt
freshly ground black pepper
olive oil

1. To make the butter, place the white wine, Rooibos and thyme in a saucepan.
   Reduce over high heat till about 45 ml remains and the mixture is syrupy in consistency.
   Leave to cool, then remove the thyme and transfer the mixture to a large bowl.
2. Add the parsley, garlic and red onion. Stir to combine.
   Place the softened butter into the bowl and mix in with an electric mixer.
   Fold in the juice and zest of the lemons and oranges. Mix in the paprika, brandy and mustard.
3. Beat in the egg yolks. Divide the mixture into three and roll into logs.
   Wrap each log in plastic wrap. Refrigerate until firm.
4. Bring a large pot of salted water to the boil. Place the crayfish in the boiling water and cook for
   about 3 minutes. Turn off the heat, leaving the crayfish in the water for a further 3 minutes.
   Remove the crayfish and allow to drain. Refresh in iced water.
5. Break off the heads of the crayfish. Use the heads to make stock.
6. Slice the tails into 2 to 3 cm slices (medallions) with a heavy knife. Season to taste.
7. Brush the medallions with olive oil and chargrill on a hot grill for about 2 minutes on each side.
8. Slice the butter logs thinly and place a slice on each crayfish medallion.
   Serve when the butter starts melting.

Serves 4

Rooibos Rub Kingklip with Rata-tea-ouille

Philippe Wagenführer

This is an ideal, light summery lunch dish.

RATA-TEA-OUILLE
200 g baby marrows, thinly sliced
200 g aubergine, thinly sliced
200 g red peppers, roasted, peeled and thinly sliced
200 g plum tomatoes, peeled, quartered,
  seeds removed and cut into petals
60 ml Rooibos-infused oil*
20 good-quality black olives, stones removed
50 g shallots or spring onions, sliced
25 ml very strong Rooibos
50 g (55 ml) butter
coarse sea salt

ROOIBOS RUB
100 g Rooibos tea leaves
20 ml honey
zest of 3 lemons
5 ml coarse sea salt
40 g dried apple, finely chopped

FISH
4 x 180 g kingklip fillets
45 ml olive oil
pinch of salt
juice and zest of 1 lemon

RATA-TEA-OUILLE

1. Place the vegetables in separate dishes and salt generously. (Keeping the vegetables separate will retain their individual, fresh flavours.) Leave to infuse for a while. When the vegetables are soft, rinse in fresh water.
2. Heat the Rooibos-infused oil in a frying pan and stir-fry the vegetables, olives and shallots very briefly, as they are already softened. Remove from the pan to a plate, retaining the juices in the pan, and set aside.
3. Return the pan to the heat. Add the Rooibos and butter to the pan juices. Boil until the liquid is reduced. Season to taste with the sea salt. When the reduction has the consistency of a rich butter sauce, return the vegetables to the pan and keep warm.

ROOIBOS RUB

4. Place all the ingredients for the rub in a blender and process to form a fine powder.

FISH

5. Just before cooking, rub one side of the fish fillets with the Rooibos rub. Heat the olive oil in a large frying pan. Place the fish, rub side down, into the pan. Make sure that the pan is not too hot, as you may burn the rub and make it very bitter. Cook for 3 minutes, then turn the fillets over and cook for a further 3 minutes or until the flesh flakes easily when tested with a fork. One minute before removing the fish from the pan, add the lemon juice and zest.
6. To serve, place the Rata-tea-ouille and its juices in the base of a heated serving dish, then top with the fish fillets.

Serves 4

* Rooibos-infused oil
  Heat 70 ml of oil over low heat with 1 Rooibos tea bag. Remove from the heat and let it stand 20 minutes to infuse. Remove the tea bag.

Rooibos Poached Norwegian Salmon on Spiced Lentils with Rooibos Infused Syrup

Nina Septoe

SPICED LENTILS

200 ml green lentils
450 ml water
salt and freshly ground black pepper
75 ml olive oil
100 g baby marrows,
    cut into bite-size pieces
50 ml diagonally sliced spring onions
25 ml finely chopped chives
50 ml finely chopped coriander
1 red chilli, finely chopped
zest and juice of 1 lemon

SALMON

400 ml water
3 Rooibos tea bags
2 cm fresh ginger, peeled and cut into julienne
2 garlic cloves, crushed
5 ml whole peppercorns
5 ml coriander seeds
720 g Norwegian salmon, cleaned and
    cut into 180 g portions

SYRUP

450 ml water
3 Rooibos tea bags
1 vanilla pod, sliced lengthways
    and seeds removed
1 red chilli, cut lengthways
300 ml white sugar

GARNISH

40 g mixed baby salad leaves
salt and freshly ground black pepper
olive oil for dressing

SPICED LENTILS

1. Place the lentils and water in a deep saucepan, season lightly and cook the lentils until al dente. Drain and rinse under cold water to ensure the lentils are completely cooled.
2. Heat a frying pan, add 50 ml of the olive oil and, once hot, add the baby marrow, season lightly and cook until golden brown but still crunchy. Drain the excess oil and cool completely.
3. In a bowl, mix the cooked lentils and baby marrow, the rest of the olive oil, the spring onions, herbs, chilli, lemon zest and juice. Adjust the seasoning if needed.

SALMON

4. Mix the water, tea bags, ginger, garlic, peppercorns and coriander seeds in a frying pan. Bring this mixture to boil, turn down the heat and infuse for about 3 to 5 minutes. Discard the teabags.
5. Place the salmon fillets into the simmering Rooibos liquid and cook about 5 to 7 minutes until medium rare (ideally the salmon should still be pink inside). Remove the fish from the liquid and set aside.

SYRUP

6. Place the water and tea bags into a saucepan, bring to boil and allow to infuse for about 10 minutes. Discard the tea bags.
7. Add the vanilla pod, chilli and sugar and bring to the boil. Cook the mixture until reduced to a syrup. The sauce should be able to coat the back of a spoon.

SERVING

8. Place a round cutter in the centre of a serving plate. Spoon approximately 125 to 190 ml of the spiced lentils into the cutter and ensure that it is firmly packed. Remove the cutter.
9. Place a piece of salmon on top of the lentils and drizzle the Rooibos syrup over the salmon and around the plate. Mix the baby salad leaves with seasoning and a little olive oil and place on top of the salmon for garnish.

NOTES:
- The green lentils can be replaced with brown lentils or chickpeas.
- Other fish can be used, such as kingklip or hake (check with the fishmonger for fish suitable for poaching and the cooking time).
- The chilli can be replaced by herbs such as parsley or dill.
- Use the vanilla seeds to flavour ice-cream or other desserts.

Serves 4

Seared Tuna with Wilted Greens & Mushrooms Served with Mussel & Rooibos Velouté

Jerome Peters

VELOUTÉ

400 g fresh mussels in shell
½ onion
10 ml chopped ginger
10 ml chopped garlic
20 ml roughly chopped fresh coriander
50 ml white wine
50 ml water
250 ml fresh cream
1 Rooibos tea bag

GREENS AND MUSHROOMS

5 ml sesame oil
100 g oyster mushrooms
100 g portabellini mushrooms
100 g shimeiji or porcini mushrooms
100 g English spinach
100 g fine green beans
100 g mange tout, julienned
5 ml black sesame seeds

TUNA

4 x 180 g tuna steaks
olive oil
salt to taste

VELOUTÉ

1. Place the fresh mussels, onion, ginger, garlic, coriander, wine and water in a hot saucepan.
2. Cook the mussels until they open, tossing regularly. Discard any mussels that did not open. Strain and keep the mussel juice and mussels.
3. Pour the mussel juice back into the saucepan, add the cream and cook to reduce to desired consistency. Remove from heat, add the Rooibos tea bag and let it stand for 2 minutes to infuse. Discard the tea bag and set aside until needed.
4. Remove the mussel meat from some of the shells, and add it to the velouté for presentation.

GREENS AND MUSHROOMS

5. Heat the sesame oil in a frying pan. Add the mushrooms, spinach, green beans and mange tout and sauté until cooked. Toss in the sesame seeds and set aside.

TUNA

6. Heat a griddle pan until smoking, brush the tuna with olive oil and season with salt.
7. Seal the tuna for 1 minute on each side (medium rare).
8. Scoop the greens and mushrooms in the bottom of serving bowls, with mussel velouté around and some shelled mussels as garnish. Then place the tuna on top. The tuna can also be sliced if desired.

Serves 4

Roberto's West Coast Mussels in Rooibos-Pernod Cream Sauce

Roberto de Carvalho

15 ml extra-virgin olive oil
1 small onion, chopped
4 medium shallots or spring onions, chopped
80 ml Pernod
500 ml strong Rooibos
4 dozen (48) fresh West Coast mussels
190 ml light cream
15 ml butter
1 ml salt
0,5 ml freshly ground black pepper

1. Heat the oil in a large, deep frying pan over medium heat.
   Sauté the onion and shallots for 2 to 3 minutes until just beginning to soften.
2. Remove the pan from the heat (to avoid a flare-up). Pour in the Pernod and Rooibos.
   Simmer for 1 minute over medium heat.
3. Add the mussels and cover the pan. Increase the heat to high.
   Steam the mussels, shaking the pan once or twice, for 5 to 7 minutes until they open.
4. Discard any unopened mussels. Using a slotted spoon, remove the mussels to a serving bowl.
   Cover with foil to keep warm.
5. With a fine-mesh strainer (or a colander lined with a large coffee filter), strain the cooking liquid
   into a medium bowl. Rinse out the frying pan and pour the strained liquid back into the pan.
   Boil over high heat for 5 to 7 minutes until the liquid is reduced to about 250 ml.
6. Reduce the heat to medium-low. Stir in the cream, butter, salt and pepper, and cook until
   heated through.
7. Drizzle the sauce over the mussels and serve.

NOTE:
To remove grit or sand that may be under the mussel shells, place them in a saucepan large enough
to hold the mussels comfortably. Dissolve about 60 ml salt in 500 ml warm water and add 30 ml
cornflour or flour. Pour the mixture into the saucepan. Add the mussels and cover with cold water.
Soak for 2 hours or overnight in the refrigerator. The mussels will expel the grit or sand.
Before cooking, rinse the mussels and scrub if scruffy looking. Snip off the 'beards' (dark threads) with
scissors. If the mussels have opened slightly before cooking, tap the shell. They should snap shut.
Discard any mussels that don't pass the tap test.

Serves 4 to 6

Pan-Fried Chicken Breast with Rooibos-Glazed Linguine and Vegetables En Papillote*

Edgar Osojnik

200 g linguine pasta
a selection of vegetables, sliced in strips
fresh herbs to taste e.g. thyme or rosemary
coarse sea salt
freshly ground black pepper
olive oil
2 chicken breast fillets
white pepper
100 ml water
1 Rooibos tea bag
10 g (10 ml) butter

1. Preheat the oven to 180 °C.
2. Bring a saucepan of salted water to the boil. Add the linguine and cook until al dente.
   Drain and set aside.
3. Place the selected vegetables on a large square of foil. Add the herbs, salt and black pepper
   and drizzle with olive oil. Wrap the foil around the vegetables to seal completely.
   Bake in the oven until al dente, about 15 minutes.
4. Season the chicken breasts with salt and white pepper. Heat a little olive oil in a frying pan
   and fry the chicken until just done. Remove from the pan and set aside.
5. To the same frying pan, add the water and the Rooibos tea bag.
   Boil briskly until the liquid is reduced by half. Remove the tea bag.
6. Add the butter and whisk. Add the linguine and toss to glaze.
7. Place the linguine on 2 plates. Slice the chicken breasts and place on top of the linguine.
   Place the vegetables on the side and spoon over the juices from the vegetable parcel.

Serves 2

* *En Papillote* (French for 'in parchment') is a method of cooking in which the food is put into a
  folded pouch or parcel and then baked. The parcel is typically made from folded baking paper,
  but other material such as a paper bag or metal foil may be used. The parcel holds in moisture
  to steam the food.

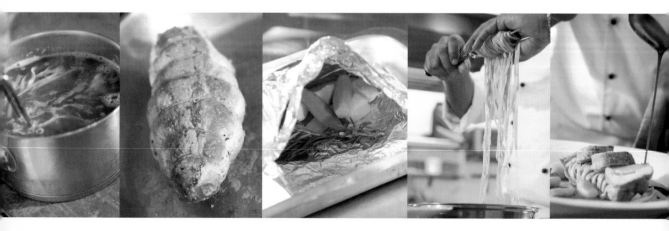

Chicken Curry

Chris Maré

1 chicken stock cube
200 ml hot, strong Rooibos
50 ml cooking oil
2 large onions, sliced
2 cloves garlic, crushed
1 piece fresh ginger, crushed
1 green pepper, seeded and chopped
10 ml curry powder
4 chicken breast fillets, cubed
1 tomato, skinned and chopped
1 tin (410 g) pineapple pieces, drained, juice reserved
salt and freshly ground black pepper to taste
cooked basmati or jasmine rice, to serve

1. Dissolve the chicken stock cube in the hot Rooibos.
2. Heat the oil in a saucepan and sauté the onions, garlic, ginger, green pepper and curry powder for 5 minutes.
3. Add the chicken and fry gently for a further 15 minutes.
4. Add the tomato, Rooibos stock, pineapple juice, salt and pepper and simmer for 20 minutes or until the chicken is tender. Stir occasionally.
5. Add the pineapple pieces and heat thoroughly.
6. Serve with fragrant basmati or jasmine rice.

Serves 4

Mini Rooibos Chicken Pot Pies
with Bacon & Marjoram

Roberto de Carvalho

5 slices smoked bacon
375 ml chopped onions
375 g whole baby carrots, peeled
250 g slender green beans, halved crossways
60 ml fresh marjoram, chopped
500 ml Rooibos Chicken Stock (see page 192)
190 ml crème fraîche
750 ml roast chicken, skin removed and coarsely shredded
freshly ground black pepper
500 g frozen puff pastry, thawed

1. Preheat the oven to 230 °C. Cook the bacon in a large, heavy-based frying pan or grill pan over medium heat until crisp. Drain the bacon on paper towels and chop.
2. Add the onion to drippings in the pan. Sauté for about 8 minutes until softened and golden. Add the carrots, green beans and marjoram. Sauté for 1 minute.
3. Add the stock. Bring to the boil over high heat. Reduce the heat to medium-high. Boil for about 8 minutes until the vegetables are almost tender and the liquid is slightly reduced.
4. Stir in 175 ml of the crème fraîche, chicken and bacon. Bring to simmer. Remove from the heat and season with pepper. Spoon the chicken mixture into 4 x 500 ml soufflé dishes.
5. Unroll the puff pastry onto a work surface. Roll out to a 30 cm square. Cut into 4 equal squares. Place the squares over the chicken mixture in the soufflé dishes. Fold the edges of the pastry over the rims of the dishes to secure.
6. Brush the tops of the pastry (not the edges) with the remaining 15 ml crème fraîche. Cut a small X in the centre of each pie lid and pierce all over with a fork.
7. Bake for about 22 minutes until the crusts are golden brown and the filling is heated through.

NOTE:
You can also make one large pot pie. Place the filling in a 23 cm diameter deep-bowled pie dish. Set the 30 cm square sheet of pastry square over the filling. Fold down the edges onto the rim. The baking time will also be about 22 minutes.

Serves 4

Ostrich Neck in Rooibos

Morné Botha

140 g (250 ml) cake flour
5 ml salt
5 ml fine white pepper
10 ml paprika
4 kg ostrich neck
125 ml sunflower oil
3 medium onions, sliced
3 leeks, rinsed and sliced
5 medium carrots, peeled and cut into chunks
2 cloves garlic, sliced
1 tin (115 g) tomato paste
1 tin (410 g) whole peeled tomatoes
5 sprigs fresh thyme
1 sprig fresh rosemary
1,5 litres strong Rooibos
750 ml red wine
750 ml strong beef stock

1. Mix the flour, salt, pepper and paprika well in a large plastic bag.
   Add the meat in batches to the bag and shake the bag to cover the meat completely with
   the flour mixture.
2. Heat some of the oil in a heavy-based saucepan. Braise the meat until well browned. Set aside.
3. Preheat the oven to 160 °C.
4. Heat the remaining oil in a large casserole. Sauté the onions, leeks, carrots and garlic in the oil
   until the onions are soft. Add the tomato paste and whole peeled tomatoes. Stir to mix.
5. Add the browned ostrich neck, thyme, rosemary, Rooibos, red wine and beef stock.
   Bring to the boil. When the liquid starts to boil, remove the dish from the heat.
   Cover it tightly with foil, replace the lid and place in the oven.
   Cook for 4 to 4½ hours until the meat is succulent and tender.
6. Check the seasoning before serving with mashed potatoes, mieliepap, rice or samp.

Serves 8

Rooibos-Smoked Springbok

Philippe Wagenführer

4 x 150 g springbok loin
15 ml freshly ground black pepper
pinch of salt
30 ml olive oil
40 g Rooibos tea leaves
10 g brown sugar
20 g wood chips
40 g sweet potato
1 egg
25 g white asparagus
25 g green asparagus
25 ml red wine
5 ml raspberry vinegar
15 ml *jus**
20 g butter

1. Rub the springbok loin with the salt and pepper. Heat 15 ml of the olive oil in a frying pan and seal the springbok on all sides.
2. Place the Rooibos tea leaves, sugar and wood chips in a large, heated saucepan.
   Insert a rack into the saucepan and place the springbok on the rack. Cover tightly with foil or another saucepan, inverted. Allow to smoke for 5 to 7 minutes.
3. Grate the sweet potato. Lightly beat the egg and stir into the grated sweet potato to bind. Heat the rest of the olive oil in a frying pan. Cook until browned and cooked through. Remove from the pan and place on a kitchen towel to absorb any excess oil.
4. Bring water to boil in a saucepan. Peel the asparagus and plunge into the boiling water to blanch. Season to taste. Sauté in the same frying pan in which the sweet potato was cooked.
5. In the same frying pan used to seal the springbok, cook the red wine until reduced, stirring to deglaze the pan. Add the vinegar and cook until the mixture is almost cooked away. Add the *jus*. Just before serving, stir in the butter to form a smooth, shiny sauce.
6. Slice the springbok and serve with the sweet potato, asparagus and a drizzle of red-wine sauce.

Serves 4

* *Jus* is French for 'juice'. It can be the juice of fruit, vegetables or meat. The term refers to a meat's own juice (a naturally occurring gravy) and not one that has to be made.

Pan-Fried Springbok with Root Vegetables

Edgar Osojnik

100 ml water
1 Rooibos tea bag
2 carrots, peeled
1 beetroot, peeled
2 parsnips, peeled
1 celeriac bulb, peeled
50 g (50 ml) butter
1 piece (350 to 480 g) springbok loin, cleaned and trimmed
salt
freshly ground black pepper
mashed potatoes for serving

1. Place the water in a small saucepan, add the Rooibos tea bag and bring to the boil.
   Simmer until the liquid is reduced to 10 ml. Remove the tea bag.
2. Cut the peeled and rinsed vegetables into cubes the thickness of a finger.
   Heat the butter in a saucepan, add the vegetables, reduce the heat and cook the vegetables
   until just cooked (do not overcook).
3. Cut the springbok loin in 2 portions. Season well with salt and pepper.
   Heat a grilling pan until hot and cook the meat until done according to taste.
4. Add the butter from the vegetable pan and the Rooibos reduction to glaze the meat.
5. Serve with the root vegetables and creamy mashed potatoes.

Serves 2

Beef & Apricot Casserole

Bushmans Kloof for Rooibos Limited

1 large onion, sliced
1 clove garlic, crushed
30 ml olive oil
2 celery stalks, chopped finely
150 g rindless bacon, diced
1 kg stewing beef, diced
40 g (70 ml) cake flour
1 tin (410 g) whole tomatoes, chopped
1 beef stock cube, dissolved in 250 ml hot, strong Rooibos
10 ml Worcestershire sauce
5 ml dried, mixed herbs
salt to taste
freshly ground black pepper to taste
250 ml red wine
125 g (200 ml) dried apricots, soaked in 250 ml cold, strong Rooibos
1 tin (285 g) whole button mushrooms, drained

1. Preheat the oven to 170 °C.
2. Sauté the onion and garlic in 15 ml of the oil until tender. Add the celery and sauté gently. Turn into a 2 litre casserole dish.
3. Fry the bacon in the remaining oil. Add to the casserole.
4. Toss the beef in the cake flour to cover. Brown the meat, in batches (add a little extra oil, if necessary). Stir in the remaining cake flour. Fry gently and add to the casserole.
5. Add the tomatoes, beef stock, Worcestershire sauce, herbs, salt, pepper, wine, the apricots with the Rooibos and mushrooms to the casserole.
6. Cover and bake for 30 to 40 minutes.

Serves 6

Rooibos Fillet

Eric Dyakopu

FILLET
4 x 200 g beef fillet
salt and freshly ground black pepper to taste
500 ml cold, strong Rooibos
4 bay leaves
10 juniper berries

FILLING
40 ml butter
2 onions, chopped
200 g portobello mushrooms, chopped
1 bunch spinach, coarsely chopped
10 peppadews, chopped
150 g mozzarella cheese, grated

POTATO GALETTE
4 potatoes, peeled and sliced in 2 mm thick slices
salt and freshly ground black pepper to taste
250 ml fresh cream
100 g Parmesan cheese, grated

SAUCE
30 ml butter
1 onion, chopped
10 Peppadews, chopped
200 ml hot, strong Rooibos
200 ml cream

FILLET

1. Season the fillet with salt and pepper, and place in a plastic container. Add the cold Rooibos, bay leaves and juniper berries, and marinate overnight. Drain the fillet, and make an incision from the one side to open it (butterfly). Keep aside.

FILLING

2. Heat the butter in a frying pan and sauté the onion until soft. Add the mushrooms and sauté until most of the liquid evaporates. Add the spinach and sauté until just wilted. Add the Peppadews and remove from the stove. When cold, mix in the mozzarella cheese.
3. Place the filling on the opened fillet, close and tie with rope or secure with toothpicks to keep its shape.

POTATO GALETTE

4. Preheat the oven to 160 °C. Place the potato slices in a greased, shallow ovenproof dish. Season with salt and pepper. Pour the cream over and sprinkle with the cheese.
5. Bake until the potato is cooked and golden brown on top.

SAUCE

6. Heat the butter in a small saucepan and sauté the onion until golden brown. Add the Peppadews and stir in the Rooibos to deglaze the saucepan. Simmer to reduce by one third. Then add the cream and season to taste.
7. Fry the stuffed fillet in a very hot griddle pan until medium rare.
8. Serve the fillet with the potato galette and the sauce. Garnish with fresh rosemary and coriander leaves.

Serves 4

Individual Lamb-Shank Bobotie with Asparagus & Roasted Red Peppers

Chris Maré

This dish goes very well with a fruit salsa, such as pineapple or peach.

BOBOTIE
olive oil for frying
2 carrots, chopped
2 onions, chopped
1 bunch celery sticks, leaves removed and chopped
1 bunch leeks, finely sliced
250 ml tomato paste
10 peppercorns
4 sprigs parsley
2 bay leaves
750 ml dry red wine
10 lamb shanks
cake flour
salt
freshly ground black pepper
3 additional onions, chopped
125 ml mild curry powder
500 ml apricot chutney

PASTRY CASES
250 g (270 ml) butter
500 g (900 ml) cake flour
1 egg, mixed with cold water
   to make 180 ml liquid
2,5 ml salt

ROOIBOS CUSTARD
300 ml cream
3 eggs
1 egg yolk
4 Rooibos tea bags

VEGETABLES
red peppers
asparagus

BOBOTIE

1. Pour a little olive oil into a saucepan and sauté the carrots, the 2 onions, celery and leeks together until the vegetables are soft. Add the tomato paste and cook until the paste is a rich, dark colour. Add the peppercorns, parsley, bay leaves and red wine.
2. Preheat the oven to 120 °C. Dust the lamb shanks in seasoned flour.
   Heat a little olive oil in a frying pan and seal the shanks on all sides.
3. Place the shanks in a deep roasting tray and add the wine mixture.
   Cover with foil and bake for 4 to 6 hours or until the meat comes off the bone very easily. Remove from the oven. When cool enough to handle, separate the meat from the bone and shred it finely.
4. Sauté the 3 additional onions in a little olive oil until translucent. Add the curry powder and cook for a few minutes. Add the shredded lamb shanks and stir in the apricot chutney. Set aside.

PASTRY CASES

5. Place the butter and flour in a food processor and mix until the mixture resembles coarse breadcrumbs. Add the egg mixture and the salt, and blend until the mixture forms a ball.
6. On a floured surface, roll out the pastry. The pastry will be used to line 10 individual moulds. Grease the moulds. Use one as a guide to cut the pastry into rings large enough to line the moulds.
7. Fill the pastry cases three-quarters full with the bobotie mixture.
8. Preheat the oven to 180 °C.

ROOIBOS CUSTARD TOPPING

9. Beat all the custard ingredients together in a small saucepan. Bring to just below the boiling point and set aside to infuse. Once cooled, remove the tea bags.
10. Top up the bobotie moulds with the Rooibos custard. Place the moulds on an oven tray and bake for 15 minutes. Remove and set aside to cool slightly. Gently remove the bobotie-filled pastry cases from the moulds.

VEGETABLES

11. Prepare the vegetables in the meantime. Roast the red peppers in the oven until the skins blacken. Remove from the oven and place in an airtight container. Once cooled, remove the skins and slice the flesh into 1 cm strips. Blanch and refresh the asparagus.
12. Serve the bobotie on top of the red peppers and asparagus.

Serves 10

Spiced Lamb & Rooibos Tortellini

Reuben Riffel

LAMB
600 g boneless leg of lamb, cubed
60 ml coarse sea salt
olive oil
2 large tomatoes, chopped
500 ml strong Rooibos
250 ml white wine
fresh thyme sprigs
zest of 2 lemons
45 ml crushed cumin seeds

TORTELLINI
500 g (780 ml) semolina flour
6 large egg yolks
water
1 extra egg yolk, beaten for brushing

GARNISH
130 g (250 ml) sultanas, soaked in
250 ml hot, strong Rooibos
250 ml Grana Padano or Parmesan
   cheese shavings

LAMB

1. Season the lamb with sea salt and set aside for a couple of minutes (some moisture will be lost, but the flavour of the lamb will intensify).
2. Heat a little olive oil in a frying pan. Seal the lamb well on all sides.
3. Place the lamb in a large saucepan. Add the tomatoes, Rooibos, wine, thyme, lemon zest and cumin. Cover and cook slowly until the lamb is soft and almost breaking apart.
4. Remove the meat from the pot. Strain the sauce and boil until reduced by half in volume. Set aside.
5. Shred the meat lightly and set aside to cool.

TORTELLINI

6. To make the tortellini, place the semolina flour into a mixing bowl.
   Make a well in the centre and add the egg yolks. Knead until the mixture is well combined.
   If the mixture is too dry, add a little water. Cover and leave to stand for 30 minutes.
   (Do not add salt to the pasta mixture. Seasoning will be added once the tortellini is cooked.)
7. Roll the pasta into sheets. Use a pastry cutter to cut out 9 cm-diameter rounds.
8. Place a spoonful of the cooked meat in the centre of each round. Brush the edges with egg and fold over to seal. Brush the folded corners with egg and press together. Place the tortellini on a floured tray in a single layer. Set aside.
9. Bring a saucepan of salted water to the boil and cook the tortellini for 2 to 3 minutes, then drain.
10. Divide among 4 bowls. Spoon over the sauce. Scatter with the soaked sultanas and Grana Padano or Parmesan shavings.

Serves 4

Lamb Potjiekos

Chris Maré

125 g prunes, stoned
1 litre strong Rooibos
25 ml oil
1 large onion, chopped
1 kg lamb knuckles
2 peppercorns
2 pimentos (allspice)
2 cloves
1 cinnamon stick
50 ml vinegar
10 ml salt
6 small potatoes, peeled and quartered
baby marrows
patty pans

1. Soak the prunes in 125 ml of the Rooibos.
2. Heat the oil in a large saucepan and sauté the onion until light brown.
   Remove from the saucepan and set aside.
3. Fry the lamb knuckles in the same saucepan until brown.
4. Return the onions to the meat in the saucepan.
   Add the whole spices and sauté for a further 1 to 2 minutes.
5. Add the rest of the Rooibos and vinegar, cover and simmer for 2½ hours.
6. Season with salt, add the potatoes and cook until almost tender.
   Then add the soaked prunes and the rest of the vegetables, and simmer until
   the meat is tender.

Serves 4 to 6

Bushmans Kloof, Cederberg

Rooibos, Lamb & Apricot Tagine

Malika van Reenen

Tagine is a North African stew, particularly popular in Moroccan cooking. The conical earthenware cooking pot in which it is traditionally prepared is also called a tagine. It is characterized by its sweet and savoury mix of flavours, often due to the use of fruits, honey or orange-flower water.

50 g (55 ml) butter
2 large onions, finely chopped
15 ml crushed garlic
1 green chilli, finely chopped
1 stick cinnamon
2 star anise
15 ml leaf masala
2 tomatoes, chopped
1 kg lamb knuckles
500 ml very strong Rooibos
100 g dried apricots, sliced
5 ml salt
25 g (30 ml) sugar
50 ml fresh coriander, chopped

1. Melt the butter in a saucepan. Add the onions and sauté until browned.
2. Add the garlic, chilli, spices and tomatoes, and cook for 2 minutes.
3. Add the lamb knuckles. Cook for about 5 minutes on medium heat until most of the liquid has evaporated.
4. Add the Rooibos and stir to mix. Cook, covered, for about 90 to 120 minutes until the meat is tender.
5. Add the apricots, salt, sugar and coriander. Mix until heated through.
   Serve with Rooibos-Scented Couscous (see page 100).

Serves 3 to 4

Rolled Pork Neck
Stuffed with Marinated Dried Fruit

Jaco Slabber

250 ml Rooibos Syrup (see page 196)
250 ml Rooibos liqueur or orange liqueur
250 g mixed, dried fruit
1 whole pork neck
salt
freshly ground black pepper
1 twig rosemary
1 clove garlic, crushed
125 ml cream

1. Pour the Rooibos syrup and liqueur into a bowl and marinate the dried fruit overnight.
2. Preheat the oven to 180 °C.
3. Debone the pork neck, taking care not to remove too much flesh as it must still be sturdy
   enough to hold the fruit. Season with salt and pepper.
4. Drain the fruit, retaining the marinade. Stuff the fruit into the pork neck,
   securing the roll with string.
5. Heat a large, heavy-based frying pan or grill pan over moderate heat until hot, and brown the pork.
   Then bake for approximately 1 hour, or until the meat juices run clear.
6. Remove the pork from the oven and set aside to rest.
7. Pour the marinade into a small saucepan and boil rapidly until the liquid is reduced to
   one-quarter of its volume.
8. Add the juices from the meat to the reduced marinade. Stir in the rosemary and garlic.
   Just before serving, stir in the cream.
9. Slice the pork neck and serve, topped with the sauce.

Serves 4 to 6

Side Dishes

*A meal accompanied by delicious side dishes
is like a beautiful woman wearing
well-chosen jewelry that complements
her looks and rounds off the perfect picture.*

Tomato Rooibos Risotto

Chantel Dartnall

ROOIBOS TOMATO STOCK
8 large, ripe Italian vine tomatoes, chopped roughly
100 g (125 ml) brown sugar
20 ml salt
2 bay leaves
1 big bunch of basil
1 sprig rosemary
2 Rooibos tea bags
3 litres cold water

RISOTTO
100 ml Gewürztraminer wine
pinch saffron
2 litres Rooibos tomato stock
olive oil
1 small onion, finely chopped
2 cloves garlic, crushed
1 bay leaf
200 g (250 ml) Arborio rice
coarse sea salt
freshly ground black pepper
2 ml brown sugar
1 bunch fresh basil
2 ml tomato paste
20 g Gruyère cheese, grated
1 tomato, cut into small dice (about 1 x 1 cm)
fresh lemon juice

ROOIBOS TOMATO STOCK

1. Place all the ingredients for the stock into a stockpot or large saucepan and slowly bring to the boil. Simmer for about 20 minutes. Strain the liquid through a chinoise or a fine-meshed sieve, lined with fine muslin cloth.

RISOTTO

2. Heat the wine and saffron in a small saucepan over a low heat to extract the colour and flavours of the saffron. Set aside.
3. Place the Rooibos tomato stock in a large saucepan and heat gently.
4. Heat 20 ml olive oil in a heavy-based saucepan. Add the chopped onion, garlic and the bay leaf and sauté for about 5 minutes on a moderate heat.
5. Add the Arborio rice to the onion. Season to taste with salt, black pepper and brown sugar. Add the fresh basil.
6. Stir in the tomato paste. Pour the saffron-infused wine into the rice mixture. Stir well to deglaze the saucepan. Cook until the wine is reduced by half. Add the heated Rooibos tomato stock, a ladle at a time. Allow each ladleful of the stock to be absorbed before adding the next ladleful. Repeat this process until the rice is tender, but still has a slight crunch (al dente).
7. Remove the bay leaf, garlic and basil leaves from the risotto.
8. Remove the risotto from the heat and stir in the grated Gruyère cheese, the diced tomato, a squeeze of fresh lemon juice, salt and black pepper. Serve immediately.

NOTE:
It can also be served as a main dish.

Serves 4 to 6

Roasted Beetroot & Rooibos Risotto

Roberto de Carvalho

3 medium beetroots, trimmed
1,5 litres Rooibos Chicken Stock (see page 192)
30 ml olive oil
1 small onion, finely chopped
400 g (500 ml) Arborio rice
125 ml dry white wine
5 ml salt
2 ml freshly ground black pepper
50 g (125 ml) Parmesan cheese, finely grated
Parmesan shavings for garnish
fresh basil for garnish

1. Set the oven rack in the centre of the oven and preheat the oven to 220 °C.
2. Tightly wrap the beetroots in a double layer of foil. Roast on a baking sheet for 75 to 90 minutes until very tender. Leaving the beetroots in the foil, set them aside for about 20 minutes until cool enough to handle.
3. While the beetroot is cooling, heat the stock in a saucepan until just simmering. Cover and keep it simmering very slowly.
4. Peel the beetroots, and discard the stems and root ends. Cut into 1 cm cubes.
5. Heat the olive oil in a wide, heavy-based saucepan. Add the onion. Sauté over moderate heat, stirring occasionally, for about 3 minutes until the onion is softened. Add the rice and cook, stirring constantly, for 1 minute.
6. Add the wine and simmer briskly. Stir constantly for a further minute until it is absorbed. Stir in 125 ml of the stock. Simmer briskly, stirring constantly, until the liquid is absorbed. Continue simmering and adding the stock, about 125 ml at a time. Stir constantly and let each addition be absorbed before adding the next, until the rice is just tender (al dente) and creamy (18 to 22 minutes). Reserve the leftover stock.
7. Stir in the beetroot, salt and pepper (the mixture will turn bright pink). While stirring, cook until heated through. Thin, if necessary, with some of the remaining stock. Stir in the grated cheese and remove the saucepan from the heat.
8. Place the risotto into 4 soup plates. Garnish with shaved Parmesan and fresh basil leaves. Serve immediately.

NOTES:
• The Parmesan must be grated very finely.
• Use a vegetable peeler to make the shavings for the garnish.

Serves 4

Rooibos Pumpkin Roll

Jaco Slabber

SYRUP
375 ml water
250 ml sugar
5 Rooibos tea bags
1 ml freshly ground nutmeg

DOUGH
250 g (460 ml) cake flour
10 ml baking powder
1 ml salt
125 g (135 ml) margarine
2 extra-large eggs
100 ml milk
apricot jam
250 ml cooked pumpkin, mashed
freshly ground nutmeg

1. Preheat the oven to 180 °C.

SYRUP

2. In a medium-sized saucepan, mix the syrup ingredients and bring to the boil, stirring, until the sugar is melted. Discard the tea bags, and pour the syrup into a rectangular ovenproof dish.

DOUGH

3. Sift the flour, baking powder and salt together in a large bowl. Cut the margarine into small cubes and rub into the flour. Add the eggs and milk, and mix well.
4. Turn the dough onto a floured surface, and roll out to a thickness of approximately 1 cm. Spread with the apricot jam and top with a layer of pumpkin pulp. Carefully roll into a roll and place it into the syrup in the dish. Dust with a sprinkling of nutmeg and bake for approximately 45 minutes.

Serves 4 to 6

'T' Quiche

Philippe Wagenführer

This quiche is the perfect accompaniment for fish. It can also be served as a main dish.

CRUST
2,5 g Rooibos tea leaves (1 tea bag)
50 g (85 ml) ground almonds
100 g (110 ml) cold butter, cut into cubes
50 g Parmesan cheese, finely grated
100 g (180 ml) cake flour
50 g hazelnuts, crushed

FILLING
500 g fresh asparagus
500 ml cream
3 Rooibos tea bags
bunch of parsley, chopped
7 eggs
500 g smooth cottage cheese
salt
white pepper

1. Preheat the oven to 160 °C.

CRUST

2. Place all the ingredients for the crust, except the hazelnuts, into a food processor and blend until the mixture forms a dough. Press the dough into the base of a quiche dish.
   Sprinkle with the crushed hazelnuts.
3. Bake for 15 to 20 minutes until the base is golden in colour. Set aside to cool.
4. Reduce the oven heat to 150 °C.

FILLING

5. Meanwhile, prepare the filling. Cook the asparagus in a large saucepan of lightly salted water until crisp-tender (do not overcook). Transfer the asparagus into a bowl of iced water to halt the cooking process. Drain on kitchen paper. Cut each asparagus stalk into 3 or 4 pieces.
6. Heat the cream over low heat. Add the Rooibos tea bags and leave to infuse for 10 minutes.
7. Remove the tea bags. Strain the cream through a sieve and pour it into a food processor.
   Add the chopped parsley and pulse until well mixed. Add the eggs and cheese. Blend until the filling has a smooth consistency. Season to taste with salt and pepper.
8. Arrange the asparagus over the crust. Cover with the Rooibos-cream mixture to a level just more than ¾ of the height of the dish, but not to the top.
9. Bake until the filling is set and moves just slightly at its centre when the dish is shaken, about 40 to 50 minutes. Do not let the filling turn too golden in colour.
10. Serve at room temperature.

Serves 6 to 8

Rooibos-Scented Couscous
Malika van Reenen

300 ml water
3 Rooibos tea bags
15 ml olive oil, plus extra for frying
5 ml salt
250 g (350 ml) couscous
1 onion, finely chopped
1 green pepper, finely chopped
5 ml crushed garlic
5 ml lemon zest
fresh coriander, chopped

1. Place the water and Rooibos tea bags in a saucepan and bring to the boil.
   Remove from the heat and leave to steep for 5 minutes. Remove the tea bags.
2. Add the 15 ml olive oil and salt and stir in the couscous.
   Return to medium heat and simmer for 2 to 3 minutes.
3. Pour a little olive oil into a frying pan. Sauté the onion, green pepper and garlic until soft.
   Add to the couscous. With a fork, stir in the lemon zest and coriander, making sure the couscous grains are separated.
4. Serve with Rooibos, Lamb and Apricot Tagine (see page 86).

Serves 3 to 4

Cape Grace, V&A Waterfront, Cape Town

Rooibos Root-Vegetable Cobbler with Chive Biscuit Topping

Roberto de Carvalho

A cobbler is a typical American pie.

ROOT-VEGETABLE FILLING

45 ml butter
1 large onion, chopped
680 g potatoes, peeled and cut into 1 cm pieces
280 g turnips, peeled and cut into 1 cm pieces
1 large carrot, peeled and cut into 1 cm pieces
7 ml chopped fresh thyme
3 ml ground cumin
2 ml freshly ground black pepper
750 ml Rooibos Chicken Stock (see page 192)
250 ml cream
300 g dried shiitake mushrooms
250 ml frozen peas
60 ml fresh chives, chopped
salt
15 ml cake flour

CHIVE BISCUIT TOPPING

280 g (500 ml) cake flour
15 ml baking powder
5 ml salt
60 ml fresh chives, chopped
90 g chilled unsalted butter, cut into
   1 cm pieces
2 large eggs, lightly beaten
125 ml full-cream milk

ROOT-VEGETABLE FILLING

1. Melt 30 ml of the butter in a large, heavy-based saucepan over medium-high heat. Add the onion and sauté for about 7 minutes until deep golden. Add the potatoes, turnips, carrot, thyme, cumin and pepper. Stir for 1 minute.
2. Add the stock and bring to the boil. Reduce the heat. Cover and simmer for about 10 minutes until the vegetables are almost tender. Stir in the cream, shiitake mushrooms, peas and chives. Season to taste with salt. Leave to simmer.
3. Mix the remaining 15 ml butter and the flour in a small bowl to blend. Stir into the vegetable mixture. Simmer for about 5 minutes until the mixture thickens slightly. Divide the vegetable mixture among 6 x 500 ml soufflé or baking dishes. Set aside. (The dish can be prepared until this stage up to 90 minutes in advance. Leave to stand at room temperature.)

CHIVE BISCUIT TOPPING

4. Preheat the oven to 220 °C. Sift the flour, baking powder and salt into bowl. Stir in the chives. Add the butter. Rub it in with the fingertips until the mixture resembles coarse breadcrumbs. Add the eggs and milk. Stir to form a soft, moist dough.
5. Turn the dough onto a generously floured surface. Knead gently until just combined. Divide the dough into 6 equal pieces. Pat each piece to an 8 to 9 cm - diameter round.
6. Place 1 round of dough on the vegetable mixture in each dish (some filling will show around the edges). Place the dishes on a large baking sheet. Bake for about 18 minutes until the topping is golden and the vegetable mixture is heated through. Leave to stand for 5 minutes before serving.

VARIATION:
It can also be prepared in a large baking dish as shown in the pictures.

Serves 6

Rooibos-Buttermilk Dumplings

Roberto de Carvalho

The dumplings can be served with stews or bredies.

250 ml buttermilk
3 Rooibos tea bags
140 g (250 ml) cake flour
50 g (90 ml) cornflour
5 ml baking powder
1 ml salt
3 ml freshly ground black pepper
30 ml cold, unsalted butter, cut into bits
45 ml finely chopped fresh chives
30 ml finely chopped fresh flat-leaf parsley

1. Heat the buttermilk and Rooibos tea bags together in a saucepan. Remove from the heat.
   Leave to infuse. When cold, remove the tea bags.
2. Sift together the flour, cornflour, baking powder, salt and pepper into a bowl. Blend in the butter
   with a pastry blender or your fingertips until the mixture resembles coarse breadcrumbs.
3. Stir in 30 ml of the chives and 15 ml parsley. Add the Rooibos-infused buttermilk, stirring just
   until the dough is moistened (do not over mix).
4. Drop 8 heaped tablespoons of the dough into simmering gravy, about 5 cm apart to allow the
   dumplings to expand. Reduce the heat.
   Cover and gently simmer for 15 to 20 minutes until the tops are dry to the touch.
5. Sprinkle the dumplings with the remaining herbs.

Serves 4

Desserts

*"I prefer to regard a dessert as I would imagine
the perfect woman: subtle, a little bittersweet,
not blowsy and extrovert.
Delicately made up, not highly rouged.
Holding back, not exposing everything and,
of course, with a flavor that lasts."*

- Graham Kerr (the Galloping Gourmet), 1960s

Emily-in-Africa Mud Pie

Johan Odendaal

CRUST
100 g ginger biscuits
100 g digestive biscuits
25 ml castor sugar
5 ml ground ginger
5 ml cocoa, sifted
70 to 90 g (75 to 100 ml) unsalted butter,
  melted and skimmed

FILLING
375 g (410 ml) unsalted butter, cubed
300 g dark chocolate (at least 50% cocoa solids),
  broken into blocks
175 g golden syrup
25 ml hot, very strong Rooibos
2 red chillies, seeded and chopped
6 extra-large eggs
25 ml cold, very strong Rooibos
150 g (375 ml) unsalted macadamia nuts,
  coarsely chopped

CRUST

1. Preheat the oven to 180 °C. Grease a 22 cm-diameter spring-form tin lightly with oil.
2. Break the biscuits into small pieces, keeping the two types separate. Place the ginger biscuits into a food processor and pulse until even, coarse crumbs are formed. Add the digestive biscuits and pulse until combined. Process until the mixture is very fine.
3. Add the sugar, ginger and cocoa, and pulse until well combined. Keep the machine running and add the butter. The mixture should just hold together when pressed between the forefinger and thumb, without being greasy.
4. Spoon half of the crumb mixture into the tin. Turning the tin on its side, press the mixture against the inside rim, forming an edging of about 1 cm. Don't bother to neaten the upper edge of the crust too much. Add the remaining crumb mixture to the tin and press evenly over the base. Place the tin on a baking tray and bake for 6 to 8 minutes. Remove and allow to cool for a few minutes. Lower the oven temperature to 100 °C.

FILLING

5. Half-fill a saucepan with boiling water and place on the stove over moderate heat. Place the butter, chocolate, golden syrup and hot Rooibos in a glass mixing bowl and set the bowl over the saucepan. Stir until the chocolate is melted and the mixture is shiny. Remove from the heat, stir in the chillies, and set aside to cool slightly.
6. Beat the eggs and cold Rooibos together. Pour the egg mixture in a thin stream into the chocolate, stirring continuously. Add half of the nuts and mix.
7. Spoon the filling into the prepared crust and sprinkle the remaining nuts over the top. Bake for 100 minutes until set, but still a little soft in the centre. Switch the oven off and allow to cool down for 30 minutes.
8. Remove the pie from the oven, allow to cool down completely, and refrigerate.
9. Loosen the ring of the tin and remove the pie. Trim the crust. Cover, refrigerate and remove 30 minutes before serving.

VARIATION:
Bake the pie in individual moulds. Line the bottoms of the moulds with the crust and line the sides with a double layer of grease proof paper. When removed from the moulds, brush the sides with apricot jam and then roll them in chopped pistachios, as shown in the pictures.

Serves 12

Rooibos, Apple, Raisin & Brioche Pudding

Reuben Riffel

BRIOCHE

250 g (450 ml) cake flour
50 g (60 ml) castor sugar
7 g instant yeast
pinch coarse sea salt
50 ml Rooibos milk (infuse a Rooibos tea bag in warm milk for 30 minutes)
3 eggs at room temperature
250 g (270 ml) soft unsalted butter, cut into blocks

FILLING

2 pink lady apples, peeled, cored and sliced
50 g (85 ml) raisins, soaked overnight in 30 ml brandy
6 eggs
500 ml pouring cream
430 ml Rooibos milk (infuse 3 Rooibos tea bags in warm milk for 30 minutes)
60 ml brandy
110 g (130 ml) castor sugar
30 ml finely grated orange zest
demerara or brown sugar

BRIOCHE

1. Combine the flour, sugar, yeast and salt in the bowl of an electric mixer fitted with a dough hook.
2. In a separate bowl, whisk the milk and eggs together. Add to the flour mixture and mix on low setting. Increase speed to high and beat for 2 to 3 minutes.
3. Add the butter, a little at a time, beating to incorporate before adding more butter.
   Beat for 1 to 2 minutes, until the dough is smooth and shiny.
4. Cover the bowl with plastic wrap and leave to stand in a warm place for 1 hour, until doubled in size.
   Preheat the oven to 190 °C in the meantime. Grease a bread tin with butter.
5. Place the dough in the prepared tin and bake for 20 to 25 minutes, until dark golden.
   Leave for 5 minutes Turn onto a wire rack to cool.
6. Lower the oven temperature to 180 °C. Slice the brioche thickly, trimming the crusts, then cut into 1,5 cm cubes. Place in a single layer on an oven tray and bake for 5 to 6 minutes, shaking the tray occasionally, until toasted and golden.

FILLING

7. Reduce the oven temperature to 160 °C. Divide the brioche cubes amongst 6 lightly buttered 1 cup-capacity ramekins, placing slices of apple and raisins between the brioche pieces.
8. Whisk the eggs, cream, milk, brandy, castor sugar and orange zest together in a bowl.
   Pour over the brioche. Leave to stand for 10 to 15 minutes so that the brioche absorbs the custard.
   Scatter with demerara or brown sugar. Bake for 12 to 15 minutes, until the custard is firm and the brioche is golden. Leave to rest for 10 minutes before serving.

Serves 6

Rooibos Malva Pudding

Mariëtte Hattingh

MALVA PUDDING
20 ml butter
210 g (250 ml) castor sugar
2 eggs
15 ml smooth apricot jam
5 ml bicarbonate of soda
125 ml lukewarm, strong Rooibos
140 g (250 ml) cake flour
1 ml salt
5 ml white vinegar

ROOIBOS CREAM SAUCE
250 ml cream
150 g (180 ml) white sugar
125 g (135 ml) butter
125 ml hot, strong Rooibos
5 ml vanilla essence

MALVA PUDDING

1. Preheat the oven to 180 °C. Grease a 1,5 litre baking tin or dish with butter.
2. Cream the butter and castor sugar together. Whisk in the whole eggs, one at a time.
   Beat well after each addition and beat until the mixture is light and foamy.
3. Stir in the jam.
4. Stir the bicarbonate of soda into the lukewarm Rooibos and then stir it into the egg mixture.
5. Sift the flour and salt together and fold it into the egg mixture. Stir in the vinegar.
6. Pour the mixture into the prepared tin or dish and bake for 45 minutes until done.

ROOIBOS CREAM SAUCE

7. Place all the ingredients for the cream sauce in a small saucepan and heat gently,
   stirring until the butter is melted and the sugar dissolved. Pour over the hot pudding.
   Cut 8 individual portions with a cookie cutter.
8. Decorate with icing sugar or spun sugar, and serve with cream sauce and berry sauce.

Serves 8

Rooibos Baked Alaska with Rooibos Sauce

Roberto de Carvalho

Invented in the 1800s, baked Alaska was a big hit in the US in the 1950s, when 'convenience' was the buzzword of the day and, despite its showy effect when served, baked Alaska is not difficult to make. Restaurants serve lavishly decorated versions under flaming cascades of liqueur, while home cooks can just bake it in the oven. Either way, the magic is there – a layer of meringue keeps the ice-cream heart from melting in the oven.

250 ml Rooibos Ice-Cream, softened (see page 122)
1 Madeira cake
4 large egg whites
1 ml cream of tartar
5 ml Amarula liqueur or nut liqueur
65 g (80 ml) sugar
375 ml very strong Rooibos
300 g milk chocolate, chopped

1. To make the cake, line a 23 x 13 cm loaf tin with plastic wrap. Leave the edges hanging over the sides of the tin. Spoon the ice-cream into the prepared tin, spreading evenly and smoothing the top.
2. Cut the madeira cake in half horizontally. Arrange one of the halves, cut side down, on the ice-cream. Place the edge against one of the sides and into one corner of the tin. Cut the remaining cake into strips. Arrange in the tin to cover the ice-cream completely.
3. Lift the overhanging plastic wrap and cover the tin. Place in the freezer for at least 4 hours until the ice-cream is firm.
4. Uncover the cake. Invert it onto a metal or other ovenproof platter. Return to the freezer.
5. Make the meringue. Beat the egg whites in a large bowl until foamy. Add the cream of tartar. Beat until soft peaks form. Beat in the liqueur. Gradually add the sugar. Beat until stiff, glossy peaks form.
6. Spread the meringue over the cake. Cover the cake completely and seal the meringue to the platter. Freeze overnight.
7. To make the sauce, combine the Rooibos and chocolate in a small, heavy-based saucepan. Stir over medium-low heat until the mixture is smooth. Increase the heat to medium. Simmer for about 2 minutes until the sauce thickens. Cool slightly.
8. Position the rack in the centre of the oven and preheat to 260 °C. Bake the dessert for about 3 minutes until the meringue is lightly browned and just set. If the oven's maximum temperature is 230 °C, bake it for 8 to 10 minutes.
9. Cut the Alaska into slices and arrange on plates. Spoon the warm sauce around the dessert and serve.

VARIATION:
Small individual Alaska's can also be made as shown in the pictures. Serve with fresh strawberries and strawberry purée.

NOTE:
The sauce can be prepared up to 3 days in advance. Keep the cake frozen. Cover the sauce and refrigerate. To serve, bake the cake as described and warm the sauce gently over medium-low heat.

Serves 6 to 8

Baklava with Rooibos Syrup

Roberto de Carvalho

SYRUP
400 g (500 ml) sugar
250 ml strong Rooibos
1 lemon, halved
1 orange, halved
1½ cinnamon sticks
170 ml honey

BAKLAVA
500 g (830 ml) whole almonds with skins, finely chopped (see NOTE)
250 g (625 ml) walnuts, finely chopped
250 g (300 ml) sugar
15 ml ground cinnamon
10 ml freshly grated nutmeg
1 ml ground cloves
1 ml salt
345 g (375 ml) unsalted butter, melted and cooled slightly
1 to 2 packets phyllo pastry (roughly 43 x 30 cm; about 28 sheets), thawed if frozen

SYRUP

1. Combine the sugar and Rooibos in a saucepan. Squeeze the juice of the lemon and orange into the mixture. Add the fruit halves and cinnamon sticks.
2. Bring the mixture to the boil over a moderate heat, uncovered. Stir occasionally, until the sugar is dissolved. Simmer for 10 minutes.
3. Stir in the honey and return to the boil. Remove the saucepan from the heat and set aside to cool to room temperature. Strain the mixture through a sieve into a large measuring cup or bowl, pressing hard to release all the syrup. Discard the solids.
4. Place the syrup in the refrigerator, uncovered, for about 1 hour until cold.

BAKLAVA

5. Place the oven rack in the centre of the oven and preheat the oven to 180 °C.
   Generously brush a baking dish (about 33 x 22,5 x 5 cm) with melted butter.
6. Mix together the almonds, walnuts, sugar, cinnamon, nutmeg, cloves and salt until combined well.
7. Halve the phyllo sheets crossways and stack the sheets. Cover the stack with plastic wrap and a dampened, clean kitchen towel (to avoid it from drying out).
8. Place 2 sheets of phyllo pastry in the bottom of the baking dish and brush the top sheet generously with butter. Continue to layer 2 sheets at a time. Stagger the sheets in each double layer slightly to cover the bottom of the dish. Brush every second sheet generously with butter, until you have used 10 sheets of the pastry.
9. After brushing the top layer of phyllo with butter, spread 375 ml of the nut mixture over it. Drizzle with 30 ml butter.
10. Repeat the layering process 3 more times. Top with 10 more sheets of phyllo. (You will use 50 half-sheets of phyllo in total.) Brush the top layer with butter. Leave the pastry to stand for 10 to 15 minutes at room temperature to harden slightly (to facilitate cutting).
11. Using a sharp knife, cut the baklava into 16 equal rectangles. Cut each piece in half diagonally. Be sure to cut all the way through.
12. Bake the baklava for 50 to 60 minutes until golden. Transfer the dish to a wire rack to cool. Slowly pour the cold syrup around the edges of the hot baklava, into all the cuts, and over the top.
13. Leave to stand at room temperature for at least 8 hours. Cover once baklava is at room temperature. Do not chill.

NOTES:
• The syrup can be made up to 5 days in advance and chilled in a sealed container.
• The baklava will keep in an airtight container up to 1 week.
• Do not chop the nuts in a food processor – this makes them release more oil, resulting in a heavier baklava.

Makes 32 pieces

Chocolate-Chip, Apple & Rooibos Soufflé

Clinton Bonhomme

400 g fresh Granny Smith apples, peeled and chopped
200 g (250 ml) granulated sugar
3 Rooibos tea bags
100 g (110 ml) butter, melted
75 g (90 ml) castor sugar
200 g egg whites (about 6 eggs)
pinch of salt
80 g good-quality chocolate, chopped
icing sugar, for dusting

1. Place the apples, sugar and Rooibos tea bags into a medium-sized saucepan, cover with the lid and simmer over medium heat to allow the liquid from the apples and tea bags to infuse. Remove the tea bags from the saucepan after 10 minutes.
2. Remove the lid and simmer until the liquid is reduced slightly (the sugar should be a straw-like colour). Remove from the heat and allow too cool. While still slightly warm, blend the mixture to form a smooth purée.
3. Preheat the oven to 190 °C.
4. Grease 6 ramekins well with the melted butter. Place 15 ml castor sugar in the base of each ramekin, shaking it around until the inside of each container is completely coated with the sugar (this will help the soufflé climb the sides of the dish during baking). Place the ramekins in the refrigerator to allow the butter to harden.
5. In a large, clean bowl, free from any oil or fat, whip the egg whites with a pinch of salt until the whites have doubled in size.
6. Weigh out 150 g of the apple-Rooibos purée. Take one-third of the egg whites and beat it into the 150 g apple-Rooibos purée to loosen it. Then fold the rest of the egg whites and the chocolate chips into the purée.
7. Scoop the mixture into the ramekins so that it is level with the rim. Run your thumb around the rim to ensure the mixture rises evenly when baking.
8. Bake for 8 minutes. Remove from the oven and dust with icing sugar.
9. Serve immediately with the Rooibos Ice-Cream (see page 122).

Serves 6

Trio of Rooibos Desserts

Chantel Dartnall

VANILLA AND ROOIBOS PANNA COTTA

JELLY TOPPING	PANNA COTTA
300 ml water	400 ml fresh cream
85 g (100 ml) castor sugar	100 ml milk
2 Rooibos tea bags	3 Rooibos tea bags
100 ml clear apple juice	1 vanilla pod
1½ gelatine leaves	85 g (100 ml) castor sugar
	2½ gelatine leaves

JELLY TOPPING

1. Place all the jelly ingredients, except the gelatine leaves, in a saucepan and bring to the boil over high heat. Simmer until the mixture is reduced by about 100 ml. Remove the tea bags.
2. Soak the gelatine in a little cold water until soft. Squeeze all the water out of the gelatine and add it to the hot Rooibos and apple liquid. Stir, and set the mixture aside to cool.
3. Pour the jelly into dariole moulds. Place in the refrigerator until the jelly has set (this will take 1 to 1½ hours).

PANNA COTTA

4. Place all the ingredients for the panna cotta, except the gelatine, in a saucepan and heat over gentle heat for about 15 minutes. Remove the tea bags and vanilla pod.
5. Soak the gelatine leaves in a little cold water until soft. Squeeze out all the water.
6. Add the gelatine to the hot cream mixture. Stir gently until well mixed. Leave the mixture to cool. Pour it onto the set jelly in the moulds, filling them to the brim. Place in the refrigerator to set.

ROOIBOS AND APPLE ICE-CREAM

300 ml milk
600 ml cream
130 g (150 ml) castor sugar
2 cinnamon sticks
3 Rooibos tea bags
5 egg yolks

1. Heat the milk, cream, half the sugar, cinnamon sticks and Rooibos tea bags in a saucepan on low heat. Remove the cinnamon sticks and tea bags.
2. Mix the egg yolks and remaining sugar with a hand mixer until light and fluffy. Keeping the mixer running, add the hot milk to the egg mixture.
3. Strain the mixture through a chinoise or fine sieve and set aside to cool. Churn in an ice-cream machine till set and keep in freezer until ready to serve.

ROOIBOS SORBET

4 x 250 ml water
340 g (400 ml) castor sugar
8 Rooibos tea bags
30 ml lemon juice

1. Place all the ingredients in a saucepan and heat over medium heat until the sugar is dissolved. Taste the mixture and add more sugar or water, if necessary. Remove the tea bags and set the mixture aside to cool.
2. Strain the mixture through a chinoise or fine sieve.
   Churn in ice-cream machine until frozen. Keep in the freezer until ready to serve.

SERVING

Unmould the panna cotta onto long rectangular plates. Scoop the ice-cream in small ramekins and the sorbet into shot glasses and arrange it on the plates with the panna cotta. Garnish the panna cotta with dried apple slices, the ice-cream with edible flowers and the sorbet with fresh apple slices.

NOTE:
If you do not have an ice-cream machine, pour the ice-cream or sorbet mixture into a shallow dish and place in the freezer for 90 minutes, stirring well at 30-minute intervals to prevent large crystals forming. Leave in the freezer until frozen.

Serves 12

Rooibos Ice-Cream

Jaco Slabber

300 ml milk
5 Rooibos tea bags
300 ml cream
7 ml vanilla essence
125 ml Rooibos Syrup (see page 196)
100 g (120 ml) castor sugar
6 egg yolks
4 egg whites

1. Heat the milk with the Rooibos tea bags until almost boiling.
   Remove from the heat and discard the tea bags.
2. Stir the cream, vanilla essence, Rooibos syrup and sugar into the milk and return
   to the heat. Stir in the egg yolks. Stirring continuously, bring the mixture almost to
   boiling point. Remove the saucepan from the heat. Set aside to cool completely.
3. Beat the egg whites until stiff. Fold into the cooled mixture. Churn in an ice-cream
   machine till frozen and keep in the freezer until serving.

NOTE:
If you do not have an ice-cream machine, pour the ice-cream mixture into a shallow dish and place in
the freezer for 90 minutes, beating well with an electric beater at 30-minute intervals to prevent large
crystals forming in the ice-cream. Leave in the freezer until frozen.

Makes about 750 ml ice-cream

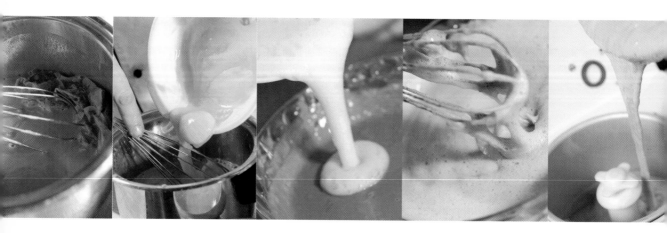

Rooibos & Berry Panna Cotta with Caramelized Oranges

Chris Maré

BERRY JELLY
2 gelatine leaves
80 g (100 ml) sugar
100 ml water
100 g frozen berries of choice

ROOIBOS PANNA COTTA
4 gelatine leaves
500 ml cream
150 g (190 ml) sugar
4 Rooibos tea bags
500 ml buttermilk

CARAMELIZED ORANGES
100 g (125 ml) sugar
3 oranges, peeled and pith removed

BERRY JELLY

1. Soak the gelatine leaves in cold water until softened. In a small saucepan, bring the sugar and water to the boil and add the frozen berries. Cook for 5 minutes.
2. Add the gelatine (without the water) to the hot mixture and mix well. Pour into the base of 6 to 8 ramekins and place in the refrigerator to set.

ROOIBOS PANNA COTTA

3. Soak the gelatine leaves in cold water until softened. Heat the cream, sugar and Rooibos tea bags in a saucepan until almost boiling. Remove from the heat, discard the tea bags and add the gelatine leaves (without the water). Stir to dissolve the gelatine. Leave to cool until the mixture starts to thicken slightly. Mix in the buttermilk. Once cooled, pour the mixture over the jelly in the ramekins and allow to set in the refrigerator.

CARAMELIZED ORANGES

4. Heat the sugar over a low heat until dissolved and a golden-brown colour (do not allow to burn). Segment the oranges, retaining the excess juice.
5. Once the sugar has caramelized, pour the excess orange juice into the pan and stir to deglaze the base. Add the orange segments and mix well.
6. Turn the panna cottas out of the moulds and place them in the centre of dessert plates. Spoon the caramelized oranges around the edges.

NOTE:
Powdered gelatine can also be used. Replace 2 gelatine sheets with 5 ml powdered gelatine.
Put 30 ml water in a small bowl and sprinkle the gelatine over the water. Leave the gelatine to swell.
First stir some of the warm liquid into the gelatine before it is added to the rest of the warm liquid .

Serves 6 to 8

Asian Pear, Cederberg Style

Philippe Wagenführer

PEARS

4 unblemished Asian or any other pears
200 g (250 ml) white sugar
475 ml hot, strong Rooibos (82 to 85 °C)
50 g piece of fresh ginger root, peeled and
  thinly sliced
zest of half an average-sized lemon
1 large mint sprig
extra fresh mint leaves to garnish (optional)

PISTACHIO CREAM SAUCE

250 ml fat-free plain yoghurt, well drained
125 ml buttermilk
15 ml pure maple syrup or honey
130 g (250 ml) pistachio nuts, shelled,
  skinned and coarsely chopped

PEARS

1. Chill 4 glasses.
2. Peel and core the pears.
3. Place the sugar, Rooibos, ginger, lemon zest and mint sprig in a medium-sized saucepan
   (large enough to hold the 4 pears in a single layer). Heat over medium heat and bring the mixture to
   just under the boil. Stir until the sugar is dissolved completely.
4. Reduce the heat to a simmer and add the pears. Cook for about 15 to 20 minutes until the pears are
   cooked but not too soft. Cool to room temperature. Cover and store in the refrigerator.

PISTACHIO CREAM SAUCE

5. Whisk together the yoghurt, buttermilk and maple syrup or honey in a small bowl. Mix in the nuts.
   Store the mixture in the refrigerator until needed.

SERVING

6. Remove the pears from the poaching liquid and drain well. Place 1 in each of the 4 chilled glasses.
   Drizzle with the sauce.
7. Garnish with fresh mint leaves, if desired, and serve immediately.

Serves 4

Rooibos & Honey-Poached Pears with Pavlova, Cardamom Cream and Rooibos Reduction

Malika van Reenen

ROOIBOS & HONEY-POACHED PEARS
10 Rooibos tea bags
1,5 litres water
250 ml honey
8 pears, peeled (keep stem intact)
80 g (100 ml) white sugar

PAVLOVA
4 egg whites
210 g (250 ml) castor sugar
8 ml white vinegar
10 ml corn flour
10 ml vanilla essence

CARDAMOM CREAM
250 ml fresh cream
1¼ ml ground cardamom

ROOIBOS & HONEY-POACHED PEARS

1. Place the Rooibos tea bags, water and honey in a saucepan. Bring to the boil.
2. Add the pears and bring the liquid back to the boil. Reduce the heat and simmer gently for 80 minutes or until the pears are soft, but still firm.
3. Remove the pears from the saucepan. Pour half of the poaching liquid over the pears.
4. Bring the remaining liquid back to the boil. Remove the tea bags. Add the sugar and boil until the liquid is reduced to a syrup. Set aside.

PAVLOVA

5. Preheat the oven to 130 °C. Line a baking tray with wax paper.
6. Using an electric beater, whisk the egg whites until stiff but not dry. Add the sugar gradually and beat until the sugar is dissolved and the mixture is very thick and glossy.
7. Sprinkle the white vinegar, cornflour and vanilla essence onto the egg-white mixture and fold in with a plastic spatula.
8. Spoon or pipe the mixture onto the prepared baking tray, making either one large Pavlova or 8 small, individual portions.
9. Bake for 60 to 90 minutes until the meringue is cream in colour on the outside, but white on the inside with a soft, marshmallowy texture.

CARDAMOM CREAM

10. Whisk the cream and cardamom together until thickened.

SERVING

11. To serve, place one pear on a plate with a Pavlova slice or individual Pavlova portion, topped with cardamom cream, and a drizzle of the Rooibos-honey reduction.

Serves 8

Rooibos Poached Pears

Eric Dyakopu

ROOIBOS PEARS

1 litre water
250 ml Chardonnay or dry white wine
2 Rooibos tea bags
170 g (200 ml) castor sugar
1 cinnamon stick
1 ml ground nutmeg
5 fresh mint leaves
4 pears, peeled

CHOCOLATE DECORATION

leaves of 1 Rooibos tea bag
50 g (125 ml) hazelnuts
4 Tennis biscuits
60 g (70 ml) castor sugar
130 g dark chocolate (70% cocoa butter)
10 fresh mint leaves, finely chopped
extra fresh mint leaves for decoration

ROOIBOS PEARS

1. Heat the water, wine, Rooibos tea bags, sugar, cinnamon, nutmeg and mint leaves in a saucepan over medium heat. Bring to the boil and cook for 2 minutes.
2. Drop the pears in the warm liquid and simmer until soft (not too soft – the pears must still keep their shape).
3. Remove the pears with a slotted spoon and let them cool.
4. Boil the liquid in the saucepan until it is reduced by a third to a syrupy consistency.

CHOCOLATE DECORATION

5. Blend the Rooibos tea leaves, nuts, biscuits and sugar together in a food processor until finely crushed.
6. Melt the chocolate in a bain-marie or in a bowl over hot water. When melted, remove from the heat and stir in the dry mixture and chopped mint.
7. Spread the chocolate mixture evenly over baking paper, about 5 mm thick.
   Place in the refrigerator until firm. Cut into triangles.
8. Cut the bottom parts of the pears so that they can stand upright. Place the pears on 4 plates and drizzle some syrup over. Decorate with fresh mint and the chocolate triangles.

Serves 4

Tea-ramisu

Morné Botha

125 ml strong Rooibos
60 ml brandy (optional – increase Rooibos if brandy is not used)
15 ml honey
1 packet (125 g) finger biscuits
3 large eggs, separated
25 g (30 ml) castor sugar
250 g mascarpone cheese
45 ml crushed almond praline or peanut brittle

1. Mix the Rooibos, brandy or extra Rooibos and honey together in a small shallow bowl.
2. Dip both sides of the biscuits into the liquid and arrange half of the biscuits in the bottom of a shallow dish, covering the base. Pour half of the leftover liquid over the biscuits.
3. Cream the egg yolks and sugar together until thick and pale. Add the mascarpone cheese to the egg mixture. Mix until smooth.
4. Beat the egg whites until stiff and fold into the mascarpone mixture.
5. Pour half of the mixture over the biscuits in the dish. Arrange the rest of the dipped biscuits on top. Pour the rest of the Rooibos and honey mixture over the biscuits.
6. Pour the remaining mascarpone mixture over the top. Sprinkle the praline on top.
7. Place in the refrigerator for at least 4 hours to set.

Serves 4 to 6

Rooibos Crème Brûlée

Luke Dale-Roberts

24 egg yolks
2 eggs
375 g (450 ml) castor sugar
500 ml milk
2 litres cream
8 Rooibos tea bags
white sugar

1. Preheat the oven to 110 ºC. Grease 12 ramekins lightly.
2. Cream the egg yolks and eggs together with the castor sugar.
3. Place the milk, cream and Rooibos tea bags in a saucepan and bring to just below boiling point (scald). Do not bring to the boil. Remove from the heat and set aside to cool slightly. Discard the tea bags.
4. Pour a little of the milk mixture into the eggs and stir well. Add the rest of the mixture and stir to blend thoroughly.
5. Strain the liquid through a fine sieve. Allow to cool completely, skimming off any foam on top.
6. Pour the mixture into the prepared ramekins. Lightly burn off any remaining foam on the tops of the brûlées using a blow torch.
7. Place in a roasting pan filled with water to reach halfway up the sides of the ramekins. Bake for 1 hour or until set.
8. Remove from the oven and leave to cool. Place in the fridge to cool completely. Dust with sugar and use a blow torch to brown the surface.

Serves 12

Rooibos Mousse with Brûlée Sauce

Jaco Slabber

ROOIBOS MOUSSE
250 ml boiling water
16 (40 g) Rooibos tea bags
100 ml milk
10 ml powdered gelatine
4 egg yolks
160 g (200 ml) soft brown sugar
350 ml cream, whipped to form soft peaks

BRÛLÉE SAUCE
6 egg yolks
90 g (175 ml) icing sugar, sifted
500 ml cream
5 ml vanilla essence

MOUSSE

1. Pour the boiling water over the Rooibos tea bags and leave to infuse for 5 minutes.
   Remove the tea bags, and add the milk and gelatine. Stir until the gelatine is dissolved.
2. In a glass bowl, set over a saucepan of boiling water, whisk the egg yolks and brown sugar together
   until thick and creamy. Remove the mixture from the heat and add the Rooibos mixture.
   Mix well and leave to cool.
3. Fold in the cream and scoop the mixture into large tea cups. Place in the refrigerator until the
   mousse has set.

BRÛLÉE SAUCE

4. Whisk the egg yolks lightly in a glass bowl. Slowly add the sugar, followed by the rest of the
   ingredients.
5. Place the mixture in a saucepan, and heat over low heat until almost boiling. Remove from the heat
   and allow to cool. Pour the sauce over the set mousse.
6. Dust with extra icing sugar and place under the grill until the sugar has caramelized.

Serves 4 to 6

Fudge Sauce with Rooibos 1

Anida van der Spuy

This sauce is delicious with vanilla ice-cream.

50 g (50 ml) butter
80 g (100 ml) brown sugar
1 tin (397 g) condensed milk
125 ml cream
200 ml strong Rooibos
pinch of salt

1. Place all the ingredients in a saucepan.
2. Heat gently, stirring constantly, until the sugar has dissolved completely.
   Bring to the boil and simmer until the sauce is thick and creamy.
   Keep on stirring to avoid sauce boiling over.
3. Cool down. The sauce will thicken to a perfect thick pouring sauce.

Makes 350 to 400 ml sauce

Rooibos Chocolate Sauce 2

Roberto de Carvalho

250 ml cream
80 g (100 ml) caramel brown sugar
3 Rooibos tea bags
450 g milk couverture chocolate*, broken into blocks
40 g (45 ml) salted butter

1. Heat the cream over low heat. Add the brown sugar and Rooibos tea bags. Infuse for 5 minutes.
   Remove the tea bags.
2. Add the chocolate and butter. Stir together gently until melted. Remove from the heat. Allow to
   cool slightly before using.

NOTE:
This sauce can be stored in the refrigerator. To use, reheat gently over a low heat.

Makes 600 ml

* Couverture chocolate has a higher percentage of cocoa butter and is also known as coating or
  dipping chocolate. Used mainly by the catering industry as it melts and coats easily, it has a glossy
  finish and intense chocolate flavour. Available at specialized sweet or baking shops. Milk chocolate
  can also be used for this recipe.

1

2

Cakes & Bakes

*Here in the Cederberg area, teatime is
Rooibos time.*
*Yet, my grandmother believed we should
never drink "bare" tea. Tea must always be
served with home-baked cakes or cookies
or melktert or koeksisters ...*

Rooibos Torte*

Morné Botha

CRUST
560 g (4 x 250 ml) cake flour
5 ml salt
10 ml baking powder
200 g (250 ml) sugar
230 g (250 ml) butter
3 large eggs, beaten

FILLING
4 Rooibos tea bags
750 ml boiling water
1 tin (385 g) condensed milk
50 g (100 ml) custard powder
50 ml milk
15 ml vanilla essence
whipped cream (optional)

CRUST

1. Preheat the oven to 180 °C. Line a baking tray with lightly greased baking paper.
2. Sift the flour, salt and baking powder together. Add the sugar and rub in the butter until the mixture resembles coarse breadcrumbs.
3. Add the beaten eggs. Mix until a dough forms. Refrigerate the mixture for a few minutes.
4. Divide the dough into 8 equal portions. Roll one piece of dough between two sheets of cling film into a round shape of about 22 cm in diameter and 3 mm thick. Repeat with the remaining dough portions. Ensure all the layers are the same size, by using a plate or the lid of a pot. Place the layers with the cling film in the refrigerator for 10 minutes.
5. Remove 1 piece of dough from the refrigerator at a time. Peel away one side of the cling film. Turn the dough onto the lightly greased baking paper. Peel away the second piece of cling film. Bake in the centre of the oven for 10 to 12 minutes or until golden.
6. Turn out onto a wire rack, remove the baking paper and leave to cool. Repeat the process with the remaining 7 pieces of dough. (The baked circles can be stored in an airtight container until needed. Place a sheet of wax or baking paper between each layer.)

FILLING

7. Place the Rooibos tea bags and boiling water in a saucepan and boil until reduced to 500 ml. Discard the tea bags.
8. Add the condensed milk and stir until smooth.
9. Mix the custard powder and milk together. Add to the heated Rooibos mixture in a thin stream and simmer until thickened. Allow to cool. Add the vanilla essence.
10. To assemble, spread 7 of the torte circles with about 100 ml of the filling each. Layer one on top of the other. Any remaining filling can be used to thicken the top layer. Crumble the 8th biscuit layer on top.
11. Store the cake overnight in a cool place to allow the crust to moisten before serving.
12. Decorate with whipped cream, if desired.

Makes 1 cake

* Tortes are Central European in origin. The most well-known of the typical tortes include the Austrian Sacher torte and Linzer torte and the many-layered Hungarian Dobos torte. An element common to most tortes is the sweet icing or filling between several cake layers.

Rooibos & Beetroot Cake

Garth Stroebel

CAKE
350 g (440 ml) sugar
220 ml oil
220 ml warm, strong Rooibos
400 g (700 ml) cake flour
pinch of salt
15 ml baking powder
4 eggs, separated
200 g fresh beetroot, cooked and grated
30 ml honey

LEMON FROSTING
500 g (960 ml) icing sugar
90 g (100 ml) butter
2 egg yolks
60 ml fresh lemon juice
5 ml fresh orange juice
10 ml finely grated lemon rind
pinch of salt

CAKE

1. Preheat the oven to 180 °C. Butter two cake tins and sprinkle with flour.
2. Mix together the sugar, oil and Rooibos until the sugar has dissolved.
3. Sift the flour, salt and baking powder together. Mix into the Rooibos mixture.
4. Add the egg yolks, beetroot and honey, and mix.
5. Whisk the egg whites until they form soft peaks, and fold into the mixture.
6. Pour the mixture into the prepared tins and bake for about 40 minutes, or until a skewer inserted into the cake comes out clean. Remove from the oven and turn out onto a rack to cool.

LEMON FROSTING

7. Sift the icing sugar into a mixing bowl and add the butter. Cream the butter and the icing sugar and gradually add the remaining ingredients. Beat to a smooth, batter-like consistency.
8. When the cake has cooled, fill with the lemon frosting and ice the top and sides with the remaining frosting. Dust with cocoa powder.
9. Cut into slices and serve.

Makes 1 cake

Rooibos & Chocolate Cake

Morné Botha

CAKE
50 g (125 ml) cocoa powder
5 ml vanilla essence
125 ml sunflower oil
250 ml very strong Rooibos
4 extra-large eggs, separated
300 g (375 ml) castor sugar
280 g (500 ml) cake flour
15 ml baking powder
2 ml salt

ICING
400 ml hot, very strong Rooibos
200 g (250 ml) sugar
45 g (50 ml) butter
20 g (50 ml) cocoa powder
25 g (50 ml) corn flour
5 ml vanilla essence
1 tin (385 g) caramel condensed milk
fresh berries and icing sugar to decorate

CAKE

1. Preheat the oven to 180 °C. Grease two spring-form cake tins (23 cm in diameter) and line the bottoms with greaseproof paper.
2. Stir the cocoa, vanilla and oil into the Rooibos until smooth. Beat the egg yolks and sugar till thick and creamy. Add the cocoa mixture to the eggs and mix well.
3. Sift the flour, baking powder and salt together. Add the cocoa mixture and beat well.
4. Whip the egg whites until soft peaks are formed and fold into the cake batter. Pour the mixture in the prepared cake tins and bake for 30 minutes or until done (when a toothpick inserted into the centre of the cake comes out clean).
5. Remove from the oven and leave to cool for a few minutes. Turn out onto a wire rack and leave to cool completely.

ICING

6. Place the hot Rooibos, sugar and butter in a saucepan. Stir to dissolve the sugar and melt the butter.
7. Mix the cocoa and corn flour with a little of the Rooibos mixture to form a smooth paste.
   Add the remaining Rooibos mixture and stir until thick. Stir in the vanilla essence. Return to the heat and boil for 2 to 3 minutes, stirring occasionally.
8. Leave to cool, then place in the refrigerator to cool completely.
9. Stir the caramel condensed milk into the chilled icing mixture and mix through. Spread half of the caramel icing on one of the layers and cover with the second layer. Spread the remaining icing on top. Decorate with fresh berries. Dust the cake with icing sugar.

Makes 1 cake

Rooibos & Walnut Carrot Cake

Edgar Osojnik

This cake can be iced with a butter or cream cheese icing if desired.

150 ml sunflower oil
2 eggs
250 g (300 ml) castor sugar
300 g (540 ml) cake flour
6 ml baking powder
10 ml bicarbonate of soda
10 ml salt
12 ml ground cinnamon
5 ml ground cloves
450 g carrots, grated
100 g (250 ml) walnuts, chopped
zest of 2 lemons
juice of 2 lemons in which 2 Rooibos tea bags have been infused

1. Preheat the oven to 190 °C. Grease a 20 cm round cake tin and line with greased baking paper.
2. Combine the oil, eggs and sugar in a medium-sized bowl.
3. In a large bowl, sieve together the flour, baking powder, bicarbonate of soda, salt, cinnamon and cloves. Add the grated carrots and stir to mix well.
4. Add the egg mixture to the carrot mixture and blend thoroughly.
5. Add the walnuts, lemon zest and lemon-Rooibos infusion and mix well.
6. Pour the mixture into the prepared cake tin and bake for about 75 minutes.
7. Leave to cool in the tin for 5 minutes. Turn onto a wire rack to cool completely.

Makes 1 cake

Rooibos Mousse Cake

Garth Stroebel

LEMON-FLAVOURED SPONGE CAKE
180 g (200 ml) butter
180 g (215 ml) castor sugar
3 large eggs
180 g (325 ml) cake flour
2 ml baking powder
pinch of salt
juice and grated zest of 1 lemon
5 ml vanilla essence

ROOIBOS MOUSSE
4 eggs
200 g (250 ml) sugar
20 ml powdered gelatine
180 ml hot, strong Rooibos
30 ml honey
juice of 1 lemon
400 ml fresh cream, whipped to soft peak stage

LEMON-FLAVOURED SPONGE CAKE

1. Preheat the oven to 180 °C. Line a baking tray (22 x 30 cm) with silicone or greaseproof paper.
2. Cream the butter and castor sugar in a mixing bowl. Add the eggs, one at a time, beating well after each addition.
3. Sift the flour, baking powder and salt together. Fold into the mixture, alternating with the lemon juice, until the mixture is thick enough to drop off a spoon.
4. Stir in the lemon zest and the vanilla essence.
5. Spread the mixture over the paper in the tin, in a 1 cm-deep layer.
   Bake in the oven for about 15 minutes or until the sponge is no longer wet to the touch.
6. Remove from the oven and leave to cool on a wire rack. Cut the sponge in half.

ROOIBOS MOUSSE

7. Whisk together the eggs and sugar until light and fluffy.
8. Dissolve the gelatine in the hot Rooibos. Add the honey and lemon juice.
   Fold the gelatine mixture gently into the egg mixture. Lightly fold in the cream.
   Spread the mixture on one layer of the sponge cake. Top with the second layer.
9. Place the cake in the refrigerator for about 1 hour to set.
10. When the mousse has set, cut it into any shape you desire, such as small rounds or triangular wedges. Decorate the shapes with chocolate fingers, sugar curls and sprigs of mint.

Serves 12

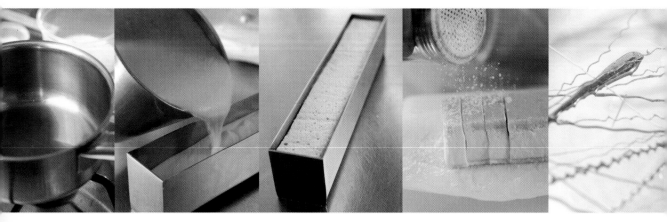

Caramel & Rooibos Cheesecake

Jaco Slabber

100 g (110 ml) butter or margarine, melted
2 packets (200 g each) Nutty Crunch biscuits, crushed
500 g cream cheese
1 tin (385 g) caramel condensed milk
250 ml Rooibos Syrup (see page 196)
20 ml caramel essence
500 ml fresh cream
30 ml castor sugar
25 ml powdered gelatin, dissolved in 50 ml warm, strong Rooibos

1. To make the biscuit crust, mix the crushed biscuits with the melted butter or margarine.
   Press the mixture into the base of a greased pie dish or loose-bottomed cake tin (23 cm diameter).
2. In a bowl, mix the cream cheese, condensed milk, Rooibos syrup and caramel essence together.
   Whip the cream and castor sugar to the soft peak stage. Add the gelatin to the cream cheese mixture
   and fold in the cream. Stir until well mixed.
3. Pour the mixture into the crust. Refrigerate for approximately 5 hours.
4. Garnish with fresh strawberries and chocolate curls.

Serves 8 to 12

Green Fig-Rooibos Tart

Jaco Slabber

2 packets (200 g each) Tennis biscuits, crushed
110 g (120 ml) butter or margarine, melted
1 tin (410 g) evaporated milk
150 g (180 ml) sugar
4 Rooibos tea bags
3 eggs, separated
15 ml powdered gelatine
250 ml green fig preserve, coarsely chopped
50 g (125 ml) mixed nuts, chopped
5 ml vanilla essence
extra green fig preserve and nuts for garnishing

1. To make the crust, mix the biscuits with the melted butter. Press the crumb mixture into a pie dish.
2. Heat the evaporated milk, sugar and Rooibos tea bags over a low heat until almost boiling. Remove from the heat and discard the tea bags.
3. Beat the egg yolks, and stir into the Rooibos mixture.
4. Return the saucepan to the heat and simmer, stirring continuously until the sauce thickens. Remove from the heat and set aside to cool.
5. When the mixture has cooled slightly, add the gelatine and stir well. Add the figs, nuts and vanilla essence. Beat the egg whites until the soft point stage and fold into the mixture.
6. Pour the mixture into the crust and place in the refrigerator to set.
7. Garnish with green fig preserve and nuts before serving.

Serves 8 to 10

Rooibos Squares

Jaco Slabber

250 g (270 ml) margarine
6 Rooibos tea bags
2 packets (200 g each) Marie biscuits, crushed
1 tin (385 g) condensed milk
250 ml glaced red and green cherries, coarsely chopped
150 ml desiccated coconut
grated zest of 1 lemon
210 g (400 ml) icing sugar, sieved
45 ml strong Rooibos

1. Heat the margarine and Rooibos tea bags over low heat until the tea bags are well saturated.
   Press the excess margarine out of the tea bags and discard the tea bags.
2. In a large bowl, mix the Rooibos-infused margarine with the biscuits, condensed milk,
   cherries, coconut and lemon zest.
3. Press the mixture into a greased cake tin of 25 x 18 cm.
4. Mix the icing sugar with sufficient strong Rooibos to make a stiff icing.
   Spread the icing over the biscuit mixture.
5. Refrigerate overnight.
6. Cut into squares to serve.

Makes about 16 to 20 squares

Rooibos Raisin Bread

Johan Odendaal

250 g (335 ml) seedless raisins, coarsely chopped
250 ml hot, strong Rooibos
100 g moskonfyt or molasses
2 extra-large eggs, beaten
10 ml wine vinegar
840 g (6 x 250 ml) cake flour
130 g (250 ml) wholewheat flour
30 g instant yeast
15 g (12 ml) salt
10 ml mixed spice
about 500 ml lukewarm, strong Rooibos
50 g (55 ml) butter

1. Place the raisins and hot Rooibos in a bowl and set aside until the raisins are plump and the Rooibos is lukewarm.
2. Grease two bread tins or 8 small pottery pots.
3. Beat the moskonfyt, eggs and vinegar together. Drain the raisins and add the raisin liquid to the egg mixture. Keep the raisins aside.
4. Sift the flours, yeast, salt and spices together in a large mixing bowl. Mix and make a well in the centre. Add the egg mixture and half (250 ml) of the lukewarm Rooibos, stirring constantly to mix well. Add more of the Rooibos (as needed) to create a soft, slightly sticky, dough.
5. Turn the dough onto a lightly floured surface. Rub the butter onto your hands and knead the dough for 10 to 12 minutes until it is smooth and elastic. Knead the dough flat and sprinkle the drained, plumped raisins on the dough. Fold the dough over the raisins to cover completely and knead for 2 to 3 minutes more.
6. Shape the dough into a ball and place it in a clean bowl, greased with a little butter. Flip the dough over in the bowl, cover with a damp cloth and place in a warm place. Allow the dough to prove for about 15 minutes, until clearly aerated, but not yet double in volume.
7. Place the dough on a lightly floured surface and knock back. Divide into 2 or 8 smaller equal portions (depending on the containers used) and shape into loaves. Place into the prepared containers and neaten the edges. Cover with a damp cloth and allow to prove until double in bulk.
8. Preheat the oven in the meantime to 200 °C.
9. Place the loaves into the hot oven and bake for 5 minutes. Lower the temperature to 180 °C and bake for a further 30 to 40 minutes.
10. Remove the loaves from the oven and turn the bread out onto a wooden board. Knock the bottom of each loaf – it should sound hollow. If not, return the loaves to the oven (without returning to the containers) and bake for a further 5 minutes. Place on cooling racks and allow to cool.

VARIATIONS:
• Add the finely grated zest of 2 oranges to the egg mixture.
• Chop 100 g (250 ml) pecan nuts or walnuts coarsely and knead into the dough once it is elastic.
• Replace the raisins with sultanas or currants.

Makes 2 large or 8 small loaves

Rooibos Health Bread

Kanya Hunt

4 Rooibos tea bags
250 ml water
250 ml buttermilk
1 jumbo egg
400 g (750 ml) wholewheat flour
100 g (250 ml) whole oats
10 ml cream of tartar
10 ml bicarbonate of soda
2,5 ml salt
100 g (180 ml) sunflower seeds
30 g (50 ml) linseeds (optional)
60 ml honey

1. Grease a 23 x 13 x 7 cm loaf tin. Preheat the oven to 180 ºC.
2. Place the Rooibos tea bags and water in a saucepan and boil for 5 to 10 minutes to make a strong infusion. Remove the tea bags. Set aside to cool.
3. Add the buttermilk and egg, and beat with a fork to mix.
4. Place all the dry ingredients and seeds, except 50 ml of the sunflower seeds and 10 ml of the linseeds, in a large mixing bowl. Make a well in the centre of the dry ingredients.
5. Pour in the honey and buttermilk-and-Rooibos mixture. Fold in lightly with a large metal spoon until just combined – the same as you would do for a muffin mixture.
6. Sprinkle some of the sunflower and linseeds in the bottom of the greased tin.
7. Spoon the bread mixture into the prepared loaf tin and sprinkle the rest of the seeds on top.
8. Bake for approximately 45 minutes.

NOTE:
Rooibos Syrup (see page 196) can also be used instead of the honey.

Makes 1 loaf

Rooibos Bran Muffins

Jaco Slabber

50 g (420 ml) bran
250 ml warm, strong Rooibos
125 g (135 ml) margarine
150 g (180 ml) brown sugar
2 eggs
500 ml buttermilk
240 g (430 ml) cake flour
65 g (125 ml) wholewheat flour
15 ml bicarbonate of soda
2 ml salt
280 g (7 x 250 ml) All Bran flakes, crushed
100 g (250 ml) pecan nuts, chopped
150 g (250 ml) raisins

1. Preheat the oven to 180 °C. Grease a muffin pan or line with pieces of baking paper.
2. Mix the bran, Rooibos and margarine and allow to cool.
3. When the bran mixture is cool, add the rest of the ingredients and mix well.
4. Fill the muffin cups half to two-thirds of their depth and bake for 30 minutes, or until a toothpick inserted into the centre of a muffin comes out clean. Turn the muffins onto a wire rack to cool.

NOTE:
The dough can be kept in the refrigerator in a tightly sealed container for 2 weeks.

Makes 18 muffins

Rooibos, Pistachio and Cardamom Biscotti

Kanya Hunt

BISCOTTI
3 Rooibos tea bags
45 ml brandy
100 g (200 ml) whole, shelled pistachio nuts
100 g (110 ml) butter, softened
125 g (150 ml) sugar
2 eggs, lightly beaten
330 g (600 ml) cake flour
5 ml ground cardamom
7,5 ml baking powder
2,5 ml salt

GLAZE
30 ml milk
sugar for dusting

1. Remove the tea leaves from the bags and soak for 30 minutes in the brandy.
2. Preheat the oven to 180 °C.
3. Roast the pistachios on an unlined baking tray, in the preheated oven for 10 minutes. Remove and cool.
4. In an electric mixer, cream the butter and sugar.
5. Slowly add the beaten eggs whilst beating continuously. Beat well.
6. Sift together the flour, cardamom, baking powder and salt, and add to the egg-and-butter mixture. Mix to form a scone-like dough.
7. Add the Rooibos infused brandy, as well as the cooled, roasted pistachios. Mix well.
8. Line a baking tray with baking paper.
9. Divide the dough into two or three equal parts and shape into rectangles of about 20 x 8 cm in size and 2 cm thick on the prepared baking tray.
10. Brush the surfaces of the biscotti dough with the milk before dusting with sugar.
11. Bake for 30 to 40 minutes until slightly risen and light brown. Remove from the oven.
12. Lower the oven temperature to 100 °C. Allow the biscotti to cool for at least 30 minutes before cutting into 1 cm thick slices.
13. Arrange the biscotti on oven racks and dry them in the cool oven for 50 to 60 minutes.

Makes 36 pieces

Rooibos Koeksisters

Kanya Hunt

For best results, start preparing the dough and syrup the night before.

KOEKSISTERS
250 ml ice-cold water
1 jumbo egg
5 ml vinegar
500 g (900 ml) cake flour
20 ml baking powder
2,5 ml salt
20 g butter

oil for frying
ice cubes for the ice bath

ROOIBOS SYRUP
1,5 litres water
3 kg (15 x 250 ml) sugar
8 Rooibos tea bags
6 star anise
2 cinnamon sticks
3 cm piece fresh root ginger
juice and zest of 1 lemon
5 ml salt
7,5 ml cream of tartar

KOEKSISTERS

1. Beat the ice-cold water, egg and vinegar together with a fork.
2. Sift together the flour, baking powder and salt. Rub the butter lightly in with the fingertips.
3. Make a well in the centre and pour in the water mixture. Combine to form a soft dough. Divide into two and knead for 10 minutes to form an elastic, firm dough. Wrap in plastic wrap and allow to rest in the refrigerator for at least 60 minutes, or best overnight.

ROOIBOS SYRUP

4. Place all the ingredients for the syrup except the cream of tartar in a large, heavy-bottomed saucepan, and dissolve the sugar over a low heat. Bring to the boil and boil for 15 minutes. Let it cool, and then stir in the cream of tartar. Place in the refrigerator overnight.

5. Roll the dough to about 5 mm thick on a surface lightly greased with cooking oil (NOT cake flour). Cut into strips and plait.
6. Heat the oil to 180 ºC. Fry the koeksisters until a deep golden brown. Drain and transfer into the ice-cold syrup bath immediately whilst still warm. Let them soak up as much syrup as possible before removing and draining on a wire rack.

NOTES:
• The secret of a juicy koeksister lies in assuring the syrup is ice cold before and during use. An ice bath works well. Some use only half of the syrup at a time, keeping the other half in the refrigerator and alternating the two batches when used.
• These koeksisters freeze particularly well.

Makes 48

Drinks

Drinks with a difference are vital ingredients of a memorable get-together ...

Rooibos Amaretto [1]

Liquid Chefs for Rooibos Limited

150 ml hot, strong Rooibos
50 ml Amaretto liqueur
30 ml chilled whipped cream

1. Pour the hot Rooibos into a glass (first place a spoon in the glass to prevent it from cracking).
2. Add the Amaretto, but do not stir. Top with chilled whipped cream and serve.

Serves 1

Rooibos Mojito [2]

Anida van der Spuy

The mojito is a Cuban classic. This recipe is with a South African twist.

30 ml Rooibos Syrup (see page 196)
60 to 80 ml white rum
2 to 3 lime wedges
a generous amount of mint leaves, without stalks
5 ice cubes, crushed
soda water

1. Place the Rooibos syrup, rum, lime wedges and mint in a tall, sturdy glass.
2. Crush the mixture with a muddler* or the back of wooden spoon.
3. Add the crushed ice and top up with soda water. Stir vigorously and serve immediately.

Serves 1

* A muddler is a bartender's tool, used to 'muddle' — or make a mash of — fruits, herbs, and/or
  spices in the bottom of a glass to release their flavour.

Rooibos 'Aqua' Martini [3]

Luke Dale-Roberts

1 shot (25 ml) Cinzano Rosso
crushed ice
1 shot (25 ml) Van der Hum or orange liqueur
4 shots (100 ml) cold, strong Rooibos
½ shot (12 ml) Grand Marnier
twist of lemon

1. Pour the Cinzano into a cocktail shaker, add the ice and shake to mix.
   Add the liqueur, Rooibos and Grand Marnier and shake.
2. Pour into Martini glasses. Garnish with a lemon twist.

Serves 2 to 3

Rooibos Martini [1]

Chris Maré

2 tots (50 ml) Rooibos Iced Tea (see page 176)
2 tots (50 ml) Absolute vodka
1 tot (25 ml) dry Martini
ice cubes
slice of lemon

1. Pour the Rooibos iced tea into a small saucepan and bring to the boil.
   Cook rapidly until the liquid has been reduced to a syrup. Set aside to cool.
2. Combine all the ingredients in a cocktail shaker. Shake well.
3. Strain the contents of the shaker through a strainer into a chilled Martini glass.
   Garnish with a twist of lemon or rosemary.

Serves 1

Rooibos Spike [2]

Liquid Chefs for Rooibos Limited

45 ml white rum
15 ml dark crème de cacao or chocolate liqueur
125 ml cold, strong Rooibos
ice

1. Mix the ingredients with the ice in a cocktail shaker.
2. Shake well and serve immediately in a highball glass.

Serves 1

Ruby Grapefruit & Rooibos Daiquiri [3]

Reuben Riffel

45 ml Bacardi white rum
40 ml fresh ruby grapefruit juice
10 ml maraschino liqueur
Rooibos-Vanilla Ice (see page 176)

1. Pour the rum, grapefruit juice and maraschino liqueur into a cocktail shaker.
   Fill with crushed Rooibos-Vanilla ice.
2. Shake hard and fast to mix. Pour into a chilled glass.

Serves 1

1

2

3

Hot Rooibos Grog 1

Liquid Chefs for Rooibos Limited

25 ml cognac or brandy
25 ml dark rum
250 ml hot, strong Rooibos
3 whole cloves
3 ml honey
pinch nutmeg
cinnamon stick to serve

1. Heat all the ingredients, apart from the cinnamon stick, in a small saucepan.
2. Serve hot with the cinnamon stick.

Serves 1

Rooibos Glühwein 2

Chris Maré

250 ml strong Rooibos
120 ml orange juice
2 oranges, cut into slices (keep the peel on)
5 ml ground cloves
2 sticks cinnamon
125 ml honey
500 ml red wine
250 ml port

1. Mix the Rooibos and orange juice in a saucepan.
2. Add the orange slices, cloves, cinnamon and honey and bring to the boil.
3. Add wine and port, and bring to the boil again, stirring constantly.
4. Strain and serve hot.

Makes about 1 litre

Irish Honey Rooibos 3

Bushmans Kloof for Rooibos Limited

lemon juice
brown sugar
200 ml Irish whisky
1 litre hot, strong Rooibos
40 ml honey

1. Dip the rims of 8 glasses into the lemon juice and then into the brown sugar.
2. Pour 25 ml of the whisky into each glass and top with the Rooibos.
3. Stir 5 ml of the honey into each glass and serve immediately.

Serves 8

1   2

3

Rooibos-Vanilla Ice 1

Reuben Riffel

Serve this ice with cocktails and home-made lemonade.
Or, blend together with banana, mango, pineapple, mineral water and ginger.
Blended with papaya, orange, lime and hanepoot grapes, it makes a delicious drink.

1,5 litres strong Rooibos
1 vanilla pod, seeds scraped

1. Mix the Rooibos and vanilla seeds together thoroughly.
2. Pour the mixture into ice cube trays. Freeze overnight.
3. Crush the Rooibos ice in an ice crusher. Alternatively, place the ice cubes in a clean tea towel, wrap and crack the cubes with a rolling pin.

Makes about 1,5 litres

Rooibos Iced Tea 2

Chris Maré

2 litres water
9 Rooibos tea bags
65 ml honey
3 whole star anise pods
1 stick cinnamon
100 g (125 ml) sugar
250 ml apple juice

1. Place all the ingredients, except the apple juice, in a saucepan and bring to the boil. Remove from the heat and set aside to cool.
2. Strain the Rooibos mixture into a jug or container. Add the apple juice. Mix well.
3. Place in the refrigerator until cold.

Makes about 2 litres

Rooibos Smoothie 3

Liquid Chefs for Rooibos Limited

500 ml water
8 Rooibos tea bags
625 ml vanilla ice-cream
15 ml lemon juice
375 ml sparkling lemon juice

1. Bring the water and Rooibos tea bags to the boil. Steep for 10 minutes. Remove the tea bags.
2. Place the Rooibos and ice-cream in a blender. Process until well-mixed. Stir in the lemon juice.
3. Pour into glasses and top up with sparkling lemon juice.

Serves 8

1

2

3

Rooibos Citrus Drink 1

Liquid Chefs for Rooibos Limited

750 ml water
6 to 8 Rooibos tea bags
50 g (60 ml) sugar
250 ml lemon or lime juice
250 ml orange juice
1 lemon or lime, sliced
1 orange, sliced
fresh mint

1. Bring the water and Rooibos tea bags to the boil.
   Remove from the heat and steep for 5 minutes. Remove the tea bags.
2. Add the sugar and stir until dissolved.
   Stir in the lemon juice, orange juice and the sliced fruit.
3. Chill in the refrigerator. Serve cold with ice and garnish with fresh mint.

Serves 8

Summer Refresh 2

Bushmans Kloof for Rooibos Limited

1 litre cold, strong Rooibos
1 litre orange juice
1 litre lemonade, chilled
500 ml soda water, chilled
1 lemon, sliced
fresh mint leaves
crushed ice

1. Mix the Rooibos and orange juice. Place in the refrigerator to chill.
2. To serve, half-fill a tall glass with the Rooibos mixture.
   Top up with the chilled lemonade and soda water to taste.
3. Garnish with the lemon slices and mint. Serve with crushed ice.

Makes 20 glasses

Iced Rooibos 1

Liquid Chefs for Rooibos Limited

1 litre boiling water
3 Rooibos tea bags
100 to 200 g (125 to 250 ml) sugar or honey to taste (optional)
freshly squeezed juice of 1 lemon
ice cubes
sliced fruit and mint leaves for garnish

1. Bring the water and Rooibos tea bags to the boil. Remove from the heat and steep for 10 minutes.
   (Sugar or honey can be added to the warm Rooibos if a sweetened iced tea is required.)
2. Remove the tea bags and allow the liquid to cool down.
3. Add the lemon juice and stir.
4. Place in the refrigerator to chill. Serve with ice cubes, garnished with fruit slices and mint.

Serves 8

Rooibos Bush Tea 2

Philippe Wagenführer

2 litres water
4 Rooibos tea bags
peel of ½ orange
peel and juice of 1 lemon
1 sprig thyme
4 stems of lemongrass, crushed
4 curry leaves (optional)
2 lime or lemon leaves
24 dried cranberries
1 chilli, seeded and diced very small
80 g (100 ml) brown sugar
12 cucumber dices (small cubes)
4 extra stems of lemongrass for serving

1. Bring the water to the boil in a large saucepan. Add the Rooibos tea bags, orange and lemon peel,
   lemon juice, thyme, lemongrass, curry leaves (if used), lime leaves, dried cranberries, chilli and
   sugar. Stir well to mix. Bring to the boil again. Remove from the stove.
2. Set aside to cool to room temperature. Strain the liquid through a fine sieve.
   Refrigerate until well chilled. Keep some of the cranberries for garnishing.
3. Place highball glasses in the refrigerator to chill. Pour the tea into the glasses.
   Garnish with the cranberries and the cucumber dice. Serve with lemongrass sticks for stirring.

Serves 6 to 8

1   2

Lemon Rooibos Detox Drink 1

Liquid Chefs for Rooibos Limited

Drink this detox drink first thing in the morning.

15 ml maple syrup or honey
freshly squeezed juice of half a lemon
pinch of cayenne pepper, to taste
250 ml hot, strong Rooibos

1. Stir the maple syrup or honey, lemon juice and cayenne pepper together in a cup.
2. Fill with hot Rooibos. Stir to mix.

Serves 1

Rooibos Latte 2

Liquid Chefs for Rooibos Limited

1 litre water
16 Rooibos tea bags
40 ml almond syrup
full cream milk
ground nutmeg or chocolate

1. Bring the water and Rooibos tea bags to the boil.
   Steep for 10 minutes to create a strong brew. Remove the tea bags.
2. Pour 125 ml hot Rooibos into each of eight cups. Add 5 ml almond syrup per cup and stir.
3. Steam the milk and top each cup with 15 ml of the steamed milk.
   Garnish with ground nutmeg or chocolate.

NOTE:
This recipe is best prepared in an espresso machine.

Serves 8

Preserves, Marinades & Stock

The people of the Cederberg know that Rooibos brings out the flavour in a dish ...

Rooibos Honey Apricots 1

Edgar Osojnik

1 litre water
400 g (280 ml) honey
6 Rooibos tea bags
4 whole cloves
2 cardamom pods
1 cinnamon stick
500 g apricots, halved and stones removed

1. Place all the ingredients, except the apricots, into a saucepan and bring to the boil.
2. Add the apricots, reduce the heat and simmer until the fruits are soft but still whole. Remove from the heat and set aside to cool. Remove the tea bags.
3. Pour the apricots and the liquid into sterilized glass jars and store in a cool dark place until needed.

Makes about 3 x 500 ml

Pineapple Rooibos Chutney 2

Edgar Osojnik

600 g fresh pineapple, cut into strips
100 ml white vinegar
5 ml curry powder
5 ml ground cinnamon
2 ml turmeric
2 whole cloves
2 cardamom pods
100 g (120 ml) castor sugar
2 Rooibos tea bags

1. Place all the ingredients in a medium saucepan and cook on a very gentle heat until the pineapple is softened. Remove the tea bags after about 10 minutes.
2. Remove the saucepan from the heat and allow the mixture to cool. Pour into a sterilized glass jar.

Makes about 500 ml

1

2

Rooibos & Apple Chutney 1

Malika van Reenen

5 Rooibos tea bags
500 ml hot water
1,5 kg Granny Smith apples, peeled, cored and cubed
2 large onions, finely chopped
1 small green chilli, finely chopped
2 large tomatoes, peeled and finely chopped
3 cardamom pods
1 cinnamon stick
2 star anise
500 g (625 ml) brown treacle sugar
1 litre white wine vinegar

1. Place the Rooibos tea bags in a bowl, add the hot water and leave to steep for 10 minutes. Remove the tea bags.
2. Place the remaining ingredients in a large saucepan. Add the Rooibos and bring to the boil.
3. Reduce the heat. Allow the mixture to simmer for 1 hour until the apples are soft and the chutney is moist and thickened.
4. Transfer the hot chutney into dry, sterilized jars. Set aside to cool.

Makes 2,2 litres

Rooibos, Lemon & Granadilla Marmalade 2

Malika van Reenen

20 Rooibos tea bags
1,8 litres boiling water
1 kg lemons
pulp of 6 granadillas
1,2 kg (6 x 250 ml) white sugar

1. Place the Rooibos tea bags in the boiling water and leave to steep for 10 minutes. Remove the tea bags.
2. Using a zester, remove all the rind from the lemons. With a sharp knife, slice the lemons into very thin strips. Place the pips and pith in a muslin bag.
3. Bring a saucepan of water to the boil. Add the sliced lemons and the zest. Allow to boil for 1 minute. Strain, discard the water and return the lemons to the saucepan.
4. Pour the Rooibos into the saucepan. Add the muslin bag containing the pips and pith (these contain extra pectin, which will help the marmalade to set).
5. Boil the mixture until most of the liquid is reduced and the lemons are soft when rubbed between the fingers.
6. Add the granadilla pulp and sugar. Bring to the boil. Reduce the heat to medium and cook for about 10 minutes until the mixture is thick and sticky.
7. Transfer the hot marmalade into dry, sterilized storage jars. Set aside to cool.

Makes 1,5 litres

1

2

Chilli Jam [1]

Jaco Slabber

Serve this jam with canapés or with bobotie instead of chutney. It is also delicious with cheese.

250 ml water
4 Rooibos tea bags
250 ml castor sugar
30 ml lemon juice
250 ml mixed chillies, sliced in thin strips
1½ gelatine leaves

1. Place the water, Rooibos tea bags and sugar in a small saucepan.
   Heat gently, stirring until the sugar is dissolved. Remove the tea bags.
2. Add the lemon juice and the chillies. Bring to the boil over a low heat, stirring continuously.
3. Simmer until the chillies begin to appear translucent. Add the gelatine leaves and stir well.
4. Remove from the heat and set aside to cool.

Makes 500 ml

Rooibos Marinade [2]

Kanya Hunt for Rooibos Limited

250 ml strong Rooibos
125 ml oil
125 ml tomato sauce
125 ml chutney
30 ml Worcestershire sauce
30 ml balsamic vinegar
3 cloves garlic, crushed
5 ml mustard powder
1 onion, chopped
1 piece fresh ginger, finely grated
30 ml brown sugar

1. Mix all the ingredients in a saucepan. Heat over moderate heat until the mixture begins to boil.
2. Simmer the mixture for 15 minutes. Set aside to cool.
3. Use to marinate red meat or chicken.

Makes about 500 ml

Rooibos Chicken Stock

Roberto de Carvalho

1,75 litres (7 x 250 ml) water
8 Rooibos tea bags
backbone and neck of 1 whole chicken
1 small onion, coarsely chopped
1 large carrot, peeled and coarsely chopped
1 large celery stalk, chopped
1 bay leaf

1. Combine all the ingredients in large saucepan. Bring to the boil.
   Reduce the heat to medium-low. Cover partially and simmer for 1 hour.
2. Strain the stock and discard the solids. Cool slightly. Chill uncovered, until cold.
   Cover and store in the refrigerator until required.

NOTE:
The stock can be made 2 days before needed.

Makes about 1,5 litres

Tasty Treats

We deserve a little treat from time to time ...

Rooibos Dressing 1

Johan Odendaal

125 ml strong Rooibos, at room temperature
125 ml extra-virgin olive oil
125 ml sunflower oil
1 extra-large egg
finely grated zest and juice of one lemon
salt to taste
dash of cayenne pepper

1. Pour the Rooibos, olive oil, sunflower oil, egg, lemon zest and juice into a mixing bowl.
   Mix with a hand-held blender (known in the trade as a 'speed stick') until emulsified.
2. Season to taste with salt and cayenne pepper. Refrigerate until needed.
3. Serve with Chicken Liver Parfait (see page 30) or salad.

Serves 12

Rooibos Syrup 2

Anida van der Spuy

2 litres (8 x 250 ml) water
5 Rooibos tea bags
50 ml honey
280 g (350 ml) white sugar
20 ml lemon juice
10 ml vanilla essence

1. Combine all the ingredients, except the vanilla essence, in a large saucepan.
   Stir over low heat until all the sugar has dissolved. Boil over moderate heat
   for 45 to 50 minutes until reduced and syrupy.
2. Remove the tea bags. Add the vanilla essence.
3. Allow the syrup to cool before using.

Makes about 300 to 350 ml

French Toast, Ricotta and Orange Rooibos Syrup

Anida van der Spuy

4 thick slices day-old white bread
4 eggs
125 ml milk
butter for frying
150 ml orange juice
zest of 1 orange
250 ml Rooibos Syrup (see page 196)
1 stick cinnamon
50 g (50 ml) butter
120 g (250 ml) ricotta cheese
50 g (125 ml) pecan nuts, chopped

1. Place the bread in a shallow bowl.
2. Whisk the eggs and milk together. Pour it over the bread and leave for a few minutes until the bread is thoroughly soaked.
3. Heat some butter in a pan. Fry the bread for 1 minute on each side. Remove to a warmed plate.
4. Mix the orange juice, zest, Rooibos syrup, cinnamon and the 50 g of butter in a small saucepan. Bring to the boil, reduce the heat and simmer until thick and syrupy.
5. Top each slice of French toast with ricotta cheese and a generous swirl of syrup.
6. Garnish with the chopped pecan nuts and serve immediately.

Serves 4

Nut & Camembert Stack with Rooibos Syrup

Anida van der Spuy

2 rounds (125 g each) Camembert cheese
4 preserved green figs, sliced
dried cranberries
pecan nuts, chopped
150 to 200 ml Rooibos Syrup (see page 196)

1. Cut the two Camembert rounds in half across the middle, creating four rounds.
2. Divide the figs, cranberries and pecan nuts in 4 and scoop it onto the cheese rounds.
   Drizzle the Rooibos syrup between each cheese layer. Stack the rounds on top of one another.
3. Decorate the top with extra fruit and nuts.
4. Pour the left-over Rooibos syrup over the Camembert stack and serve with savoury biscuits.

Serves 4

Rooibos Quince Jelly Mould

Jaco Slabber

quinces
castor sugar
Rooibos Syrup (see page 196)
brandy

1. Preheat the oven to 180 °C.
2. Rub the quinces with a cloth to remove the outer woolly coating.
   Pack the fruit in a baking tray or oven dish and cover with foil.
3. Bake the quinces for about 90 minutes, or until soft. Remove from the oven and set aside until cool enough to handle.
4. Cut the fruit in half and remove the pips. Purée the quinces with their skins still on.
5. Weigh the pulp. In a saucepan, mix the fruit with half its weight in castor sugar and half in Rooibos syrup. Add 5 ml brandy for each 1 kg of fruit. Mix well.
6. Heat the mixture over a low heat, stirring continuously until the sugar is melted. Boil for approximately 30 minutes until the mixture is dark in colour. Pour the quince pulp into a lined square tin and set aside to cool and harden.
7. Cut in slices and serve with a selection of cheeses after a meal.

Index